spl ffs

A CELEBRATION OF ULTURE

D0892335

spl/ffs

A CELEBRATION OF CANNABIS CULTURE

Chrysalis
Impact

First published in 2003 by Chrysalis Impact
An imprint of Chrysalis Books plc
The Chrysalis Building, Bramley Road, London, W10 6SP

A member of **Chrysalis** Books plc
© 2003 Chrysalis Books plc

ISBN 1 84411 009 5

Text © Nick Jones
Volume © Chrysalis Books plc 2003

Commissioning editors: Will Steeds, Chris Stone
Project editor: Adam Ward
Photography: Neil Sutherland
Designed by Grade Design Consultants, London
Colour reproduction: Anorax Imaging Ltd.
Printed and bound in Italy
Additional text by Mick Farren and Laura Ward
Illustrations on pages 100-121 from *The Joint Rolling Handbook* published by Bobcat Press.

The Publishers would like to thank

Contents

Foreword

I have taken cannabis almost every day for the last 38 years and still love smoking loads of well-rolled joints. The first was so enjoyable that I smoked another one (and another one). Soon, I was buying so much, I couldn't smoke it all, so I became a dealer, then a smuggler. It was a wonderful life:

I visited over 50 countries with as many passports, was extremely rich, and had dealings with organizations as diverse as the mafia and the British secret services. I have no regrets. But I wouldn't recommend such a career to anyone not wishing to live a large part of their life behind bars. I spent nine years in some of the toughest prisons in the world. Released in 1995, I was instantly rehabilitated by a hefty advance to write my autobiography, *Mr. Nice*, which I did with fellow elderly hippies in mind as potential readers. I was, therefore, truly astonished to discover that its unexpected best-seller status was primarily due to its popularity among people several decades younger than I was. Through a plethora of media interviews and several public book readings, it became clear that the predominant reason why so many adolescents and university students read and enjoyed *Mr. Nice* was their frustration with the law prohibiting cannabis consumption and trade. Until then, I had no idea of the extraordinary extent of cannabis use by young people today.

Swamped by the spotlight of media attention, I determined to use my skyrocketing notoriety in as responsible a way as possible, doing whatever I could to hasten the day that cannabis would be re-legalised. The enemy is the average politician, who seems to be either too stupid to realise the damage caused by prohibition or too morally bankrupt to speak against the party line. With this in mind, I decided to stand for Parliament at the British General Election in 1997. Needless to say, I was not elected by any of the four separate constituencies in which I stood. Next, I applied for the job of Drug Czar. Again, I was unsuccessful, but I will carry on trying to legalise cannabis until I die or it happens. And to ensure there will always be plenty of strains, I have established the Mr. Nice Seed Bank.

Several publications about cannabis have emerged since *Mr. Nice*; but unlike so many of them, this book by Chrysalis Impact is for the real enthusiast and is most certainly 'A Celebration of Cannabis Culture' in all its forms. It covers everything from a most interesting and comprehensive narrative history of cannabis to its role in present day cultures, particularly those of music, film, and magazines. The sections on joint-rolling and strains of grass and hash are a real delight and include some wonderful photographs. There's a very useful guide to the coffee shops of Amsterdam. And for those of you who don't smoke, there's the chapter called 'The Munchies.'

Well written, beautifully illustrated, and a very good mix of content, this book is as fun to read as it is informative.

Howard Marks

Howard Marks
www.mrnice.net

Introduction

There is nothing quite as wonderful as rolling and smoking a spliff.

First there is the exquisite ritual and anticipation of building it: the delicate origami of pasting the papers together; the cooking and crumbling of the hash or the grinding of the grass; the leisurely rub to achieve consistency of mix; the coiling of the cardboard roach; the firm yet gentle rolling action; the gentle licking of the adhesive strip and the final flamboyant flourish of twisting the touchpaper.

After the first few drags, your mood mellows, your body relaxes and you are enveloped in a comfortable glow of well-being.

Take a couple more tokes and the sense of well-being spreads deliciously throughout your body. Depression lifts, spirits rise, problems dissolve, cares and troubles magically evaporate. The fog of uncertainty lifts and suddenly you can see the way forward mapped out clearly and calmly before you…

Wonder drug

Thomas Forcade, the maverick founding editor of the *High Times* magazine, once observed, 'I never met a drug I didn't like, but I like pot the best.' He had a good point. Cannabis has a lot to recommend it over other drugs. One of its greatest plus points, of course, is that is has none of the unpleasant side effects of hard drugs. It's non-addictive and you can smoke it to your heart's content without any danger of developing a craving habit or waking up in the middle of the night in a cold sweat.

Then there is its endless variety. Other drugs are dull and monotonous by comparison. One snort of coke is very much like any other and the only way of judging it is in terms of its strength and level of purity. Not so with cannabis. Quite apart from the different ways in which it can be prepared – dried in its natural form as grass or threshed and pressed to create hashish – there are an infinite number of different types of marijuana out there, each with its own unique flavour, appearance and high. As the cannabis chronicler Jason King memorably put it, 'Cannabis grows in every imaginable shade of colour, with infinite shapes, flavours, aromas

Right: The all-too-rare sight of a bushy hemp plant growing in a field, in this instance in Ontario, Canada.

and effects. I have tasted more flavours in marijuana than in food.'

Potheads thus enjoy the pleasures of connoisseurship denied to other drug users. And, like fine wine drinkers, they can lay down cannabis cellars, selecting particular strains to suit particular moods and occasions. Furthermore, when their palates become jaded and the high starts succumbing to the law of diminishing returns, novelty and potency can be restored by the simple expedient of switching cannabis 'brand' or type; each different variety providing a subtly different slant on reality.

Nor does the cornucopia of cannabis end there. For there are nearly as many different ways of smoking the stuff as there are different types. Quite apart from variations on the spliff theme, affording dedicated dope smokers endless scope for invention and experimentation, there is also a panoply of pot-smoking paraphernalia out there, from pipes and chillums to elaborate bongs and high-tech vaporisers. It really is a case of whatever turns you on.

Cannabis has proven medical applications too. Its analgesic and sedative properties have long been recognised, while recent research has also established its credentials as an effective way of alleviating symptoms ranging from glaucoma through to anorexia, AIDs and multiple sclerosis.

Eco-friendly

Apart from its psychoactively rich female flowers, cannabis can also be farmed for hemp – a crop with impeccable ecological credentials. It's extremely hardy – as one would expect from a plant that started life as a weed – and its cultivation requires the use of no harmful pesticides. It is a highly efficient crop too and absolutely nothing is wasted. Its seeds can be crushed to obtain oil, while its fibrous husks can be used in the manufacture of hard-wearing clothing, canvas and paper – a fact that has prompted many environmentalists concerned at the destruction of the world's rainforests to hail hemp as an obvious alternative to fulfil the world's paper needs.

Shape of things to come

The aim of this book is to explore and celebrate cannabis in all its myriad manifestations. It has travelled a very long way from its Central Asian homeland where it first caught early man's attention growing as a troublesome weed. Since then its seeds have come to be scattered all over the world and it has succeeded in lodging itself into every nook and cranny of our collective consciousness and culture.

We owe an incalculable debt to cannabis. This book is intended to recognise that debt and thereby partially repay it. I hope that in reading it you derive at least a modicum of the pleasure I took in writing it.

Right: Marijuana starter plants are cultivated at Positronics, a marijuana grow shop, in Amsterdam in 1996.

"It is possible that a certain amount of brain damage is of therapeutic value."

Dr Paul Hoch

Chapter 1

Roots

"Dam, mara dam, Shiva. Bom Shankar, bom Shiva."

("High, so high, Shiva. Hail Shankar, hail Shiva.")

Ritual sadhu chant when firing up a chillum

Roots

**Cannabis is the botanical name given to Indian hemp –
a wonderfully versatile plant that has been of great
service to man for thousands of years. References to the
plant first crop up in China around 3000BC and much of
its early history revolves around Central Asia and
northern India, where it is thought to have originated.**

The plant's uses are manifold. Its fibrous stems are the perfect medium from which to make paper, cloth and rope, while the flowers and resinous leaves of its female plants have long been valued medically for their various analgesic, anaesthetic, antispasmodic and antidepressant properties

These same flowers and leaves, with their high concentration of the psychoactive ingredient tetrahydrocannabinol (THC), have a long history of recreational use, too.

There are three distinct types of cannabis plant: *sativa*, *indica* and *ruderalis*. *Cannabis sativa* is much bushier and taller than *Cannabis indica* and both are traditionally cultivated for their high THC contents. *Cannabis ruderalis*, on the other hand, tends to be a lot stringier and weedier.

It possesses only a minimal THC content and is primarily cultivated for its fibre.

Hash or grass
The two main cannabis preparations for getting high are marijuana and hashish. Marijuana is made up of the dried but otherwise untreated female flowers and leaves of the female plant, whereas hashish is made by pressing the resin powder, which is first extracted from the dried female flowers by threshing or sieving.

Both hashish and marijuana have acquired various other names around the world over time. Marijuana, for instance, becomes grass in the US and Britain or ganga in India. Hashish, meanwhile, is often referred to as pot in the

Green in the house – a modern grow room.

western world or as charas in India.

However, whatever you want to call the stuff, the psychological effects of consuming cannabis for recreational purposes remain the same the world over, namely euphoria, distortions of space and time with consequent loss of short-term memory, as well as mild delusions and hallucinations. Although there is no indication of cannabis being physically addictive, prolonged heavy use has been known to produce a mild psychological dependency.

Of the two preparations, hashish is often the more potent because, in its purest form, it contains the most THC, whereas marijuana is an unrefined product in which the THC-rich resin glands are mixed up with a lot of non-psychoactive vegetal matter.

As hashish is refined from raw marijuana, its use as a means of getting high would have been predated by that of marijuana.

Pot luck

How early man discovered the cannabis plant's psychoactive properties in the first place requires little imagination. He was probably out foraging for the edible seeds among its flowers, got sticky fingers, gnawed the resin off with his teeth and got mightily blasted as a result.

Proper hashish – systematically hand-pressed – would not have appeared on the scene until later when man had become more settled and had started cultivating the land. Possibly a sheet of cloth would have been used to thresh out the seeds from the flowers of the dried plants. A thin layer of resin gland dust would have remained amid the leaf and flower debris, which, if flapped out onto a fire, would have produced a beguiling aroma and a heady high among those breathing in the fumes.

The next step would have been to introduce a form of sieving to obtain a purer resin dust. Hand rubbing would have followed – an extremely laborious process with even the most dexterous worker being hard pushed to produce more than 50g (1¾oz) a day. However, in the early days, this would have been the only method available. The more sophisticated process of sieving dried cannabis pollen through muslin and then pressing it between plates was probably not developed until as late as the 17th century.

Genetically-engineered green

The precise origin of hashish is lost in the smoke of time, but again it would probably have first been produced in its Central Asian or northern Indian homeland. However, these have always been politically volatile regions where accurate early records are scarce and where most of our impressions have been shaped by a heady blend of myth, religious bias and folklore.

Of course, prior to man entering the equation, cannabis would have been a wild plant. Only after its usefulness had been recognised would the wild seeds have been collected and the plant systematically cultivated. As it began to be farmed for specific purposes – fibre, drugs, etc – selective breeding would have been introduced

"prolonged heavy use has been known to produce a mild psychological dependency"

Right: Seeds of weed.

to best bring out those qualities the farmer was after. However, a farmer cultivating for, say, hemp fibre would have had a completely different set of criteria to one cultivating it for medical or recreational use. Hence, an early form of genetic engineering would have developed whereby fibrous strains were grown for hemp production, while heavily flowering varieties that were rich in resin would have been earmarked for medical or recreational uses. As this system developed, harvests and seeds would have begun to be traded and the plant's diaspora would have become more accelerated.

Dig it

Speculation regarding the geographical home of cannabis hovers around Central Asia and northern India. Linnaeus – the 18th-century Swedish founding father of modern botany – originally classified *Cannabis sativa*. He believed it to be indigenous to northern India.

However, later research by the Russian botanist Nicolai Vavilov in the 1930s pinpointed it as originating from the Samarkand area north of Afghanistan and the Hindu Kush. It was Vavilov, too, who claimed credit for first identifying *Cannabis indica* – a distinct Afghani strain of the plant – as opposed to the more prevalent *Cannabis sativa*, which was found in northern India.

Traces of cannabis in the form of cloth, resin and seed have been discovered at various archaeological sites throughout Central Asia and

northern India, suggesting that its use in one form or another has been endemic to these regions for many thousands of years. However, the earliest archaeological evidence comes from Chinese sites dating back several thousand years BC. Hemp rope marks have been discovered on pieces of pottery from the period, while fragments of hemp-based cloth and paper have also been unearthed. It took the Arab world a further 800 years to discover paper and the Europeans 1,200 years – which just goes to show how cannabis can be said to have a truly civilising effect on people.

As early man further explored the plant's versatility, new facets and uses continued to unravel and soon its use as a staple crop began spreading like wildfire.

Most early cloth used as bed linen, clothing, tents, rugs, carpets or towels would have been made of hemp. The Greek historian Herodotus, writing in 450BC, compares hemp clothes favourably with those made of flax linen, remarking, 'None but a very experienced person could tell whether they were of hemp or flax.'

Nothing would have been wasted and even worn out hemp cloth would have been recycled to produce paper.

The seeds, too, proved multi-functional. They could be used as a nutritious foodstuff in baking or casseroles. They could also be used as bird feed and fish bait and, when pressed, produced an oil that proved particularly effective when burned in lamps to provide illumination.

reference to the medical use of cannabis dates from 700BC when the Persian prophet Zarathustra gave the drug top-billing in a list he compiled of more than 10,000 medicinal plants. The plant also went on to figure prominently in a Chinese medical treatise 200 years later.

Scythian stoners

However, in terms of the recreational use of cannabis, it is the Scythians who emerge as the likeliest candidates for ranking as the world's first potheads. Records suggest that they were systematically cultivating the plant to get stoned in southern Siberia from as early as 700BC. They might well have been responsible, too, for introducing the Indians and Persians to the delights of cannabis culture.

The Scythians' ritualised use of the drug is well documented by Herodotus writing, around 500BC. He describes how they rigged up primitive smoking chambers, draping hides over sticks to make Heath Robinson mini-tents into which they would take it in turn to poke their heads to inhale the smoke snaking from trays of burning cannabis embers. He reports how such acts excited them to 'cries of exultation'. Nor was it just the Scythians firing it up. Herodotus describes the antics of another tribe in the area who liked to party around cannabis bonfires. 'As it burns,' he writes, 'it smokes like incense, and the smell of it makes them drunk, just as wine does us ... They get more and more intoxicated until finally they jump up and start dancing and singing.'

Filipino hemp fibre ready for export. Hemp remains a key crop in many parts of the world.

Early medicine, too, utilised every aspect of the plant, from its roots, stem and branches through to its leaves, buds and seeds. The first written

The holy herb

Religion has proved one of the prime catalysts in spreading the gospel of ganga. This is perhaps hardly surprising considering the close affinity between the euphoric effects of cannabis and the ecstasy of religious fervour.

Of the major world religions, it is only Christianity that has been a bit of a party pooper by consistently denying the divinity of the weed. The Spanish Inquisition actually went so far as to outlaw the use of cannabis in the 12th century on the grounds that it was an instrument of the occult – a move endorsed by Pope Innocent VIII in 1484 when he denounced it as the work of the devil and placed a papal ban on it.

However, Hinduism has always embraced the drug wholeheartedly and it crops up fairly frequently in its religious mythology, particularly in connection with Shiva – the Hindu god of destruction.

Legend has it that one day Shiva came across Krishna bathing in the Ganges and was so incensed with jealousy at Krishna's beauty that he fired off an arrow at him. It found its mark but was not fatal. The wounded Krishna clambered out of the river to safety and the first ganga plant is said to have sprouted from a spot on the bank at which a drop of his divine blood fell.

Shiva was later resting in the plant's shade and began nibbling at its leaves. So impressed was he with the effects that he adopted the plant as his

Left: A sadhu partakes of the chillum.

talisman and thereby became the patron saint of potheads.

Ganga and charas continue to be used as a sacrament by his followers – the dreadlocked and nomadic sadhus who are to be found wandering the religious pilgrimage routes criss-crossing India. Sadhus traditionally carry only three possessions: a trident, a begging bowl and a chillum. And to this day they continue to make an annual pilgrimage each summer to the sacred cave of Amrinath, high up in the Kashmiri Himalayas, which they believe to be the birthplace of Shiva. Once gathered together they religiously fire up enormous clay chillums in honour of the great god of ganga.

Thus smoked Zarathustra

Nor is it only the Shivites who revere cannabis as a sacrament and its use has become common-place in many mainstream Hindu ceremonies including births, deaths and marriages.

Pot has also played a pivotal role in Buddhist culture. The princely Siddhartha – the original Buddha – lived exclusively on a cannabis diet prior to finding enlightenment beneath a banyan tree in the 4th century BC. And cannabis continues to be used as a sacrament by various Chinese, Tibetan and Nepalese Buddhist sects to this day. Indeed, the highly prized Nepalese Temple Balls are so named precisely because of their ritualised use within Buddhist monasteries.

Nor has the use of spliff in religious rituals been restricted exclusively to Hindus and

The Cult of the Assassins

The word 'assassin' derives from 'hashishin', meaning hashish eater. This was the name given to an 11th-century cult of Ismaili hitmen based high up in the mountains of modern-day Iran.

Accurate records of the cult are scarce, its early history shrouded in mystery and steeped in blood. But the 19th-century French Arabist scholar Sylvestre de Sacy opined, 'I have no doubt that the denomination was given to the Ismailis on account of their using an intoxicating liquid or preparation still known in the East by the name of hashish.' The cult was founded and ruled by Sheikh Hasan ibn al-Sabah – a Persian Ismaili who claimed royal Arabian blood. Popular folklore nicknamed him the Old Man of the Mountains. Such were Hasan's guerrilla skills that, in 1090, he successfully stormed the well-

nigh impregnable fortress of Alamut, nestling high amid inhospitable mountain peaks at more than 10,000ft (3,000m) and commanding a bird's-eye view of the main trade route between the Caspian coast and the Persian highlands.

Hasan used Alamut to train a crack squad of young warriors. He conscripted them locally and demanded total commitment from them while preparing them for suicide missions.

The traveller Marco Polo describes how Hasan first doped and then secretly transported these young men into a garden of earthly delights within the walls of Alamut as part of their initiation. 'He kept at his court a number of youths of the country from 12 to 20 years of age, such as had a taste for soldiering... Then he would introduce them to his garden some four, six, or ten at a time, having first made them drink a certain potion which cast them into a deep sleep, and then causing them to be lifted and carried in...

'When therefore they awoke, and found themselves in a place so charming, they deemed that it was paradise in very truth. And the ladies and damsels dallied with them to their hearts' content.'

With the sweet taste of hashish still on their lips and with Hasan's teachings that death was an illusion still ringing in their ears, the fledgling assassins would then be duly dispatched on various murderous missions. They were promised that, whatever the upshot, they would be returned triumphant to their hashish paradise.

The assassins regarded themselves as Ismaili freedom fighters, but neighbouring warlords and politicians branded them highwaymen and terrorists after a series of politically high-profile assassinations rocked the Arab world.

Western Crusaders of the time likewise brought back terrifying tales of infidel savages who knew no fear. Typical of these was one supplied by a Frenchman, Count Henry of Champagne, who visited Alamut in 1194 and experienced their valour at first hand. By his account, Hasan ordered two of his men to hurl themselves off the castle's ramparts as a sign of loyalty, which they duly did and with predictably gory results.

The cult went on to survive the death of Hasan and continued to be the scourge of Persia and neighbouring Arab states. Hasan was succeeded by several other leaders at Alamut before the mountain stronghold was finally stormed by marauding Mongolian hordes in 1256. During the next 20 years, the cult became something of a spent force, homeless and dispossessed.

The heyday of the assassins was now over, although scattered pockets of the cult can still be found today in parts of Iran, northern Syria and India. However, it would seem that they have been put out to graze as there have been no recent reports of any assassinations perpetrated by them.

Their leader, to whom assassins continue to pay a tithe of ten per cent of their earnings, is the Aga Khan – hereditary head of the Ismaili sect, direct descendant of the last leader at Alamut and one of the richest men on earth. The revenue from his scattered following of hashish-fuelled assassins is no doubt swallowed up by his lavish lifestyle of jet-setting between sporting tournaments in Paris, New York and London. It is a subject of some speculation whether the Aga Khan still enjoys the odd puff himself for old time's sake.

Buddhists. It has also had a major influence on Islamic culture. Although not specifically mentioned in the Koran, cannabis was adopted as a sacrament by the Islamic Zoroastrian priests of the 6th and 7th centuries BC. Followers of the prophet Zarathustra, these zonked-out Zoroastrians, or Magi as they were also known, exerted a major influence on Islamic mysticism in Central Asia at the time and may well have been responsible for turning on the Persian Sufi Muslims to the pleasures of the weed.

Persian folklore doesn't actually back this theory up, instead accrediting the discovery of cannabis to a Sufi monk called Sheik Haidar. Haidar is said to have lived a life of quiet contemplation in the remote northern mountains of the country. One day, while out walking, he came across a thicket of marijuana plants gently swaying and rustling in the breeze. Attracted by their pungent aroma, the monk began picking and nibbling at their resinous flowers. The next thing he knew he was as high as a kite. And as the Sufis, like the Zoroastrians, equate divine revelation with the feelgood factor, the monk automatically came to the conclusion that this beautiful buzz was a gift from god. From that day on, Haidar became a lifelong convert to the wacky weed and soon attracted a following of like-minded doped-up disciples who, on his death, honoured his memory by planting a marijuana garden around his tomb. This became a shrine to visiting Sufi pilgrims who were intrigued by the cannabis and the effect it had on the monks who tended the garden. For, instead of being sombre, as one might expect under the circumstances, these monks were constantly cracking jokes and having a good time. So the pilgrims picked up the pot habit too and spread the spliff gospel when they returned home to their friends and families in Damascus and Egypt.

Hashish eating went on to become all the rage in Egypt. Indeed, the Garden of Cafour near Cairo was specifically set up as a resort at which hashish-heads could chill out until it was destroyed by Islamic fundamentalists in the 13th century.

Yet another splinter group from Sheik Haidar's sect set up a Sufi colony on the Malabar coast of India where they preached the gospel of the sacred weed and actively promoted getting high.

Baba Ku

Meanwhile, across the border from Persia in neighbouring Afghanistan, hashish aficionados have their own version of Sheik Haidar in the shape of a character called Baba Ku. So striking are the similarities between the stories of Sheikh Haidar and Baba Ku that they probably originate from the same source. Like Haidar, Baba Ku is characterised as a devout Sufi. He is celebrated for first bringing hashish to Afghanistan; he and his followers consumed the drug in prodigious quantities, regarding it as both a divine sacrament and a medicine. Baba Ku is generally acknowledged to be the founding father of cannabis culture in Afghanistan, and he is traditionally depicted as puffing on a giant hubble-bubble pipe. Again paralleling the Haidar legend, on the death of Baba Ku his disciples set up a shrine to him in the town of Balk in northern Afghanistan where they continued to cultivate a plot of cannabis in his memory. Pilgrims to the site were encouraged to smoke it up big time.

Indeed, to this day in Afghanistan there are still hashish babas who venerate Baba Ku. Like the sadhus of India, they generally shun possessions other than their stash of hash and lead nomadic lives. However, from time to time they will gather together in smoking fraternities – summoned by a single mournful note blown through a giant conch shell – to fire it up in remembrance of the great Baba Ku. These Afghani hashish babas are some of the most serious smokers on earth and have been known to get through as much as an ounce (28g) per head at a single sitting.

Another Islamic country strong on cannabis folklore is Morocco. Although a relative infant in terms of hashish production, the Moroccans have long been renowned for their love of kif – a marijuana and tobacco blend traditionally smoked in pipes. And they too have their patron saint of pot in the form of Sidi Hiri. Yet another Sufi Muslim, Sidi Hiri is said to have originally come to Morocco from Algeria bringing the sacred herb with him. Legend has it that he led a nomadic existence, sleeping rough in caves, wandering round the country, reciting the Koran, getting righteously ripped and turning on the locals to the joys of ganga.

The dope diaspora

The popularity of cannabis as a recreational drug received a major boost in the late 14th century thanks to Tamburlaine the Great. The scale of Tamburlaine's conquests were awe-inspiring – stretching all the way from Mongolia right through to the Mediterranean. Tamburlaine changed the whole political complexion of the area and opened up totally new trade routes. And wherever he and his marauding troops went they took cannabis with them.

Vast tracts of land around Tamburlaine's Samarkand HQ were devoted to cannabis cultivation while he was also directly responsible for introducing the crop to certain key areas of Afghanistan, India and Nepal. His sphere of influence did not end there and he made additional marijuana inroads throughout the Middle East and Africa too.

Cannabis, meanwhile, had already reached Europe with the Moorish Muslim occupation of Spain in the 8th century. Eight hundred years later, Christopher Columbus set sail for the New World and hard on his heels came the conquering Spanish conquistadors who pioneered the cultivation of cannabis for hemp in the Americas.

Nor was the traffic just one way – the Old World may have given the New World cannabis but the Old World reciprocated by yielding up its precious tobacco crops. The histories of these two weeds – dope and tobacco – have since become inextricably entwined. The global craze for tobacco that followed its discovery by the Europeans significantly widened the appeal of cannabis smoking and fanned the enormous increase in its international trade that later blossomed.

This period also marked the heyday of European maritime history – a time of voyages of discovery and huge sea battles. Hemp products proved particularly well suited to the needs of seafaring vessels. Apart from the sails, all of the rigging, ropes, nets and flags would have been made from hemp, as well as the oakum sealing agents used to protect the wooden timbers from the ravages of salt water.

Such was the importance of hemp in these times that when the British navy's access to it in the East Indies was cut off by the Dutch in the late 16th century, King James I ordered his North American colonists to start growing it. Hemp soon became a staple crop on the East Coast and in Virginia where farmers failing to grow it incurred fines.

Weed out west

Indeed, as the hemp historian Jack Herer has pointed out, cannabis played a key role in early North American history. The Declaration of Independence was printed on hemp paper, while the cowboy pioneers of the Wild West travelled in convoys of hemp-covered wagons, no doubt praying that their Red Indian enemies were back home in their wigwams puffing on their cannabis-packed peace pipes rather than lying in wait to ambush them round the next corner. And

later still, during the famous Californian gold rush of 1849, the prospectors wore the original Levi jeans, manufactured from riveted hemp and with heavy-duty pockets strong enough to withstand the bags of heavy gold dust they were hoping to stash in them.

Nor did the multi-functionality of the marijuana plant end there. Thickets of hemp were often used agriculturally to act as windbreakers or to stem soil erosion, while hemp fibres were used in the manufacture of insulating panels that were both fire and noise resistant.

Let the good times roll

Although hemp products were well established on both sides of the Atlantic by the early 19th century, European and American interest in the plant's medical and recreational potential was a little slower to take off.

French soldiers first encountered dope smoking during Napoleon's campaign in Egypt in 1798. Bonaparte issued a blanket ban but this was studiously ignored both by the Egyptian locals and his own troops who ended up taking the practice back to France as a souvenir.

The appearance of the new drug captured the interest of the French medical establishment and by the 1840s various cannabis preparations had become readily available over the counter in many of the capital's pharmacies. Its recreational use also caught on and even became rather chic following the formation of Le Club des Hachichins – a hashish-eating society which

The French army during Napoleon's campaign in Egypt, 1798.

attracted the cream of the French artistic establishment.

At the same time as the French were discovering the joys of hashish through their colonial interests in Africa, their British colonialist counterparts were coming across it in India. The Indians had already developed a highly sophisticated distribution network for cannabis long before the British arrived. Trade in both charas and ganga was taxed and tightly regulated, being channelled through official government shops. The bulk of the charas was imported from Turkestan at that time, while most of the ganga was being domestically cultivated, mainly around Bengal.

Victorian potheads
However, unlike the decadent French in Egypt, there is little evidence to suggest that many members of the British Raj went native, forgoing their gin and tonics in favour of charas and ganga. Nevertheless, these strait-laced colonialists were astute enough to scent the profit opportunity presented by cannabis and set about regulating and taxing it with an even greater rigour than the Indians had done previously.

Back in Blighty, meanwhile, the pharmaceutical industry came up with several commercially produced cannabis tinctures which enjoyed a limited success – most famously Queen Victoria was prescribed one of them to help cope with her chronic PMS pains. However, opium was a great deal more popular, both medically and recreationally, and cannabis in Victorian England never acquired the cachet it had achieved across the Channel.

Le Club des Hachichins
The psychoactive properties of hashish were first brought to the attention of the French public by

Doctor Jacques Joseph Moreau. Using himself as a guinea pig, he researched and published two highly influential papers on the drug's effects in the early 1840s.

Apart from the hashish horrors of paranoia and alienation, Moreau also described the delicious and exhilarating dreams and hallucinations he underwent while under the drug's influence.

The poets Charles Baudelaire and Pierre Jules Théophile Gautier got to hear of Moreau's work. They were greatly intrigued. Hashish was new, exotic and Oriental – in fact perfectly in keeping with the decadent aesthetic they were attempting to develop at the time. Enlisting the guidance and support of Moreau – the Doctor Feelgood of his day – they established monthly meetings of Le Club des Hachichins (the Hashish Eaters' Club) in the sumptuous salons of the baroque 17th-century Hotel de Lauzan on the Ile St-Louis in Paris's bohemian Latin Quarter. Other distinguished members of the club included the painter Eugène Delacroix and the novelist Alexandre Dumas. Honoré de Balzac and Victor Hugo were among other leading literati of the day to make occasional visits.

Blissed-out bibliophiles

With so much literary talent on tap, records of the club's meetings make for fascinating reading. Gautier, in particular, penned a fabulously atmospheric account of the club's very first meeting. His arrival at the Hotel de Lauzan is pure Hammer horror, 'The rusty old bolt opened and the door of massive planks turned on its hinges.' Once inside, Gautier relates how Dr Moreau presented him with a silver spoonful of hashish, whispering conspiratorially, 'This will be deducted from your share in Paradise.' Then, as the hash begins to kick in, Gautier notes how suddenly 'everything seemed larger, richer, more splendid...The water I drank became the most exquisite wine, the meat, once in my mouth, became strawberries, the strawberries, meat. I could not distinguish a fish from a cutlet.'

He notices, too, that one of his dining companions had slumped back in his chair, 'his eyes unseeing and his arms inert,' and how he 'let himself drift voluptuously in the bottomless sea of nothingness.' Exclamations such as 'What bliss!', 'I'm swimming in ecstasy' and 'I'm plunging into the depths of delight' ring out among the blissed out bibliophiles.

As the evening progresses, Gautier describes how the initial assault on his senses subsides and mellows into a sense of contented well-being: 'The air caressed about me in a thousand voluptuous whirlpools; a delectable apathy took hold of me and spilled me on to the sofa.' He feels as if his body is dissolving and becoming transparent, with phantasmagorical waves of sound and colour washing over it. But the poor poet has been lulled into a false sense of security and his calm is soon shattered by a series of

Right: A hashish den in New York, 1925.

"Dr Moreau presented him with a silver spoonful of hashish, whispering conspiratorially, 'This will be deducted from your share in Paradise'"

terrifying hallucinations. Glancing into a mirror – always fatal for the seriously stoned – he sees he has been transformed into a blue elephant. Things go from bad to worse with the onset of severe paranoia. It is not until Gautier reaches home that he finally emerges, exhausted and shell-shocked, from his hashish oblivion.

Fellow poet and club habitué Baudelaire was actually living in the Hotel de Lauzan at the time, so at least he didn't have far to crawl home after these monthly binges. He likewise wrote at some length about his experiences there, likening the effect of hashish to a magnification of real life and the everyday. He writes how lights and colours take on an added intensity and how senses become scrambled. 'Hashish always invokes magnificences of light, splendours of colour, cascades of liquid gold... Sounds cloak themselves with colours; colours blossom into music.'

Le Club des Hachichins marks a very important milestone in the history of cannabis. For it is through the jottings and journals of Baudelaire, Gautier, Moreau and the others that we recognise the first proper Western analysis of the drug and its effects. Potheads of the Western world owe them a distinct debt of gratitude. They planted the seed that was, over the next century and a half, to develop and blossom into the fully fledged flower power of the 1960s.

Left: Hotel de Lauzan – once home to Le Club des Hachichins.

The Hotel de Lauzan has changed greatly over the years. Today the Mayor of Paris uses it to host grand receptions and banquets for polite society. No longer do cries of ecstasy and terror echo along its corridors. However, some of the Mayor's more sensitive guests have been known to remark on the ghostly whiff of hashish still hovering in the air.

State of the Union

The biggest impact cannabis made on the English-speaking world at this time was in North America. A plethora of pot products began appearing in American pharmacies, including cannabis-laced cigarettes, which were said to work wonders for asthmatics by opening up their bronchial tubes.

Its recreational use also caught on. The New York writer Fitz Hugh Ludlow – a friend and contemporary of Mark Twain – had been intrigued by reports of Le Club des Hachichins in Paris and determined to embark on some research of his own. He kept a journal of his experiences with cannabis tincture which he went on to publish in book form in 1857 as (*The Hasheesh Eater*) – a fantastical and somewhat overblown work that nevertheless went on to enjoy a posthumous cult status.

Pot pioneers

America's passion for pot was further stoked by Philadelphia's Centennial Exposition of 1876. This featured a Turkish Hashish Pavilion, visitors to which were invited to partake of a puff on a hookah. The attraction proved a roaring success with crowds flocking there. Word spread like wildfire and the fashion fast caught on. Within a decade no self-respecting American city was without a hashish den. Apart from Philadelphia, smoking fraternities sprang up in cities as far afield as Chicago, St Louis, New Orleans, New York and Boston. By the 1880s it was estimated that there were more than 500 such establishments in New York City alone.

An article in an 1883 issue of *Harper's* magazine described one of them. Its tone was sensationalist, dwelling on how the smokers were attired in slippers, silk dressing gowns and tasselled hats, and how they reclined comatose on divans, pandered to by sinister foreign servants. They were portrayed as being literally out of their minds, lost in dreams, engaged in animated conversations with themselves and staggering around blindly, subject to senseless fits of giggles and hallucinations. It concluded breathlessly, 'Truly it was the cradle of dreams rocking placidly in the very heart of a great city, translated from Baghdad to Gotham.'

The conspiracy against cannabis

American cannabis consumption was to change dramatically over the next 50 years as marijuana came to replace hashish as the preparation of choice. It was probably the early African and Indian immigrants to the continent – pawns in the great colonialist game – who first turned on the Caribbean and South America to smoking grass.

From there the practice would have travelled up through Central America and Mexico, finally arriving in Texas at around the turn of the century. Grass was probably first brought into Texas by 'wetback' workers seeking to escape the grinding poverty of Mexico. The habit caught on, spreading among the poor and dispossessed to such an extent that, by 1914, smoking grass had become relatively commonplace among the Hispanics of El Paso and New Orleans.

This was all happening in the immediate aftermath of the Spanish-American War when US public opinion was virulently anti-Hispanic. It was an obvious strategy for the newspapers of the day to extend the fear and loathing in which Mexicans were held to their practice of smoking weed.

So a smear campaign was launched featuring stories of Hispanic hopheads running amok and perpetrating the most horrendous and bloodthirsty crimes while high on grass. One by one, states started enacting laws against the drug: first it was California, then Texas, soon followed by Louisiana, New York and others.

But author and hemp activist Jack Herer believes this was just the tip of the iceberg. In his book *The Emperor Wears No Clothes* he spins out a conspiracy theory in which this press scaremongering masked another and more sinister hidden agenda – namely the total eradication of hemp cultivation in the US. And he names and shames Harry Anslinger as being

Harry Anslinger, one of the prime movers in the move to outlaw cannabis.

the prime mover in this Machiavellian plot. Anslinger was undoubtedly an experienced propagandist and political opportunist. He had cut his teeth in law enforcement during the 1920s alcohol prohibition years. However, getting wind of the fact that the days of alcohol prohibition were numbered – it was finally repealed in 1933 – Anslinger began looking around for another job, which was supplied by his uncle Albert

Mellon (who was then serving in President Hoover's government). Uncle Albert got his nephew appointed founding director of the Federal Bureau of Narcotics (FBN) in 1931, from where he was to wage a relentless war against the weed for the next 30 years.

Vested interest

It has been suggested that Anslinger only got this plum job because his Uncle Albert shared banking interests with the giant DuPont corporation. DuPont had made its money from munitions during the First World War. However, since then the company had been forced to diversify. One of the ways it did this was by becoming a major player in oil-based synthetic fibres such as nylon. However, advances being made in the US hemp industry at the time were threatening to render redundant the need for such synthetic fibres.

DuPont's extensive paper mill interests were likewise being threatened by the development of increasingly successful hemp-based alternatives. Other businesses also stood to suffer. Randolph Hearst – the ruthless press baron immortalised by Orson Welles in *Citizen Kane* – likewise had extensive paper mill interests that he would have wished to protect.

So, Herer and his fellow conspiracists argue, the burgeoning hemp industry had to be stopped

Left: Movie propaganda? A poster for *Reefer Madness* implores America to 'Wake up'.

"They become bestial demonics with the mad lust to kill"

in its tracks. However, to do so openly would have provoked public outcry. So a little subterfuge was called for – namely the demonisation of dope smoking.

The groundwork had already been laid by the smear campaign in the press, particularly among Hearst's stable of titles. This was now built upon by Anslinger and his cronies at the FBN who perpetuated the myths appearing in the papers. Indeed many of the more lurid newspaper stories were simply recycled to become ammunition in the FBN's own propaganda campaign. Typical of these was one produced by the Universal News Service in 1936, which remarked, 'Those addicted to marijuana, after an early feeling of exhilaration, soon lose all restraints, all inhibitions. They become bestial demoniacs with the mad lust to kill...' Other gruesome and sensationalist stories of dope-fuelled depravity included black men raping white girls, fathers raping daughters and mad axe killers wiping out

"The Narcotics Section recognises the great danger of marijuana due to its definite impairment of the mentality and the fact that its continuous use leads direct to the insane asylum"

Harry Anslinger, Commissioner of Narcotics, 1938

entire families. They all provided grist to the mill for Anslinger's campaign, as did the grisly pictures of savagely beaten and horribly mutilated victims.

Nor was it just the FBN and the newspapers. A plethora of pulp fiction and trashy movies was pumped out with such lurid titles as *Assassin Of Youth*, *Weed With Roots In Hell* and – the undisputed classic of the genre – *Reefer Madness*.

The campaign against cannabis was even taken up by certain sections of the Church, with bible-bashing ministers preaching from their pulpits about the wickedness of the weed and the perils of pot smoking.

Marijuana tax bill

It was in this climate of largely media-manufactured hysteria that the Marijuana Tax Bill was enacted in 1937. While falling short of positively outlawing the cultivation of hemp, the bill nevertheless taxed the trade in it so heavily as to make it prohibitive. It is thus, the conspiracists argue, that the unholy trinity of corrupt government, big business and gutter journalism won the day. The burgeoning American hemp industry – so full of unrealised promise – had effectively been stopped in its tracks and was never to recover.

But that was to be by no means the end of the story in the war against the weed. When Anslinger finally retired from the FBN in 1962 he had just 400 agents working under him. By the time he died 15 years later, the FBN had become

the Drugs Enforcement Agency (DEA) boasting a sophisticated network of 10,000 agents worldwide. Conspiracy theories apart, for this achievement alone Anslinger must rank as one of the biggest party poopers of all time and as public enemy number one in the pothead hall of shame.

Bush doctors

'Glory be to the father and to the maker of creation. As it was in the beginning is now and ever shall be world without end. Jah Rastafari. Eternal God Selassie I.' Such is the ritual invocation with which the dreadlocked Rastafarian brethren of Jamaica fire up their bonfire spliffs of 'the holy herb'.

Ganga is the lifeblood of rastafarianism and its use by the cult as a sacrament is justified by biblical references such as 'Thou shall eat the herb of the field' and 'He causeth the grass to grow for cattle, and the herb for the service of man.'

But for all its reliance on biblical texts, Rastafarianism is a relatively recent phenomenon, the roots of which can be traced directly back to Marcus Mosiah Garvey – one of Jamaica's most famous sons and founder of the Back to Africa movement which proposed repatriation for the scattered descendants of African slaves. Garvey was born in the village of Saint Ann in 1887 and became a national hero for his championing of black civil rights. Garvey developed an idealised notion of Africa – a continent he never actually visited. But for Garvey and his followers Africa became what

Zion was to the Jews; the promised land of milk and honey to which they would one day return triumphant.

There was no space in Garvey's scheme of things for the white man, with his colonial ambitions and slave-driving ways and he became the movement's bogeyman. Garvey's rallying cries were 'Africa for the African' and 'Look to Africa for the crowning of a black king, he shall be the redeemer.'

King of kings

These words seemed prophetic to his scattered followers when, in 1930, Tafari Makonnen – who claimed direct descendancy from King David, King Solomon and the Queen of Sheba – was crowned King of Kings, Lion of the Tribe of Judah and Emperor Haile Selassie of Ethiopia. This event reignited excitement among Garvey's splintered former supporters and brought them together in Kingston, Jamaica, by 1934 as an identifiably Rastafarian cult believing in the divinity of Haile Selassie. The debt to Garvey was made specific by their adoption of his Back to Africa flag with its red, gold and green colours said to represent respectively the blood of black martyrs, the riches of their African homeland and the holy herb of the sacrament.

While there is no evidence to suggest that either Garvey or Selassie were themselves tokers, between them they undoubtedly, if unwittingly, spawned a movement that went on to become a byword for the excessive use of marijuana.

"there is no evidence to suggest that either Garvey or Selassie were themselves tokers"

As the movement gained momentum in the ghettos of Kingston, it took on a distinctly anti-establishment flavour which duly attracted the attention of the authorities. One of its more vocal founders, Leonard Howell, was arrested on charges of sedition and inciting racial hatred. He was sentenced to two years. On his release, Howell and a band of followers decamped from Kingston and headed for a remote and inaccessible range of hills about 20 miles away, where they set up a commune in the mountain wilderness called Pinnacle.

It was at Pinnacle that the signature dreadlocks first appeared. And it was at Pinnacle too that the rastas were first enabled to indulge their passion for both cultivating and smoking ganga on a more lavish scale, away from the prying eyes of the authorities. Sociologically, the ritual use of ganga by the rastas satisfied two distinct needs: the need to protest; and the need for spiritual fulfilment. By smoking his weed, the rastaman could both flaunt the despised laws laid down by white colonialists – 'Babylon', in rasta-speak – and at the same time achieve oneness with himself and god. The excessive smoking of ganga has since become de rigueur at all rasta ceremonies and gatherings.

The local hill farmers had long been doing the same as the rastas, using their more inaccessible 'crown lands' for ganga cultivation. This made perfect sense as the more remote the gardens were, the less likely they would be to be discovered by the overstretched rural police. The size of such plantations varied from small patches to bigger commercial operations financed by city moneymen. The impoverished farmers would jump at the chance of taking a cut of the profits of a commercial harvest, which to them would represent a fortune and would more than compensate for the risks involved.

The Pinnacle experiment didn't last. Its downfall was due to the greed of some of its

Left: Reggae legend Bob Marley relaxes with a spliff.

members who started extorting protection money from the impoverished local farmers. Word got back to the Kingston authorities who busted Pinnacle in 1941, again imprisoning Howell and several dozen of his followers. The rastas returned to their mountain eyrie on their release but were again raided in 1954. This time, though, the police razed the commune to the ground and, rather than going to the expense of gaoling the troublesome rastas again, simply dumped them back in the slums of Kingston to fend for themselves as best they could. Shortly after, Howell declared himself a divinity, thereby losing the support of his fellow rastas, and he was later committed to a local mental hospital.

However, in other ways, the soil of the ghetto proved conducive to the Rastafarian movement and its numbers grew. The first Rastafarian convention, known as a Nyabingi, was held in Kingston in 1958. Nyabingis still continue to be a feature of the Rastafarian calendar and are regularly convened to celebrate special occasions such as the birthdays of Marcus Garvey and Haile Selassie. Often lasting several days or even up to a week, they are traditionally high spirited, featuring prayers, music, dancing and the smoking of copious amounts of the sacred herb.

The first Nyabingi in 1958 was a crucial date in Rastafarian history, attracting hundreds of marijuana-toking brethren. The air was thick with the smoke of the holy herb as the rastas beat drums and danced around hastily improvised bonfires. Inevitably, there were clashes with police and even an ill-fated attempt by a militant splinter group to liberate the city in the name of Haile Selassie.

Present at this first Nyabingi was the Reverend Claudius Henry, a conman cleric. Sensing an opportunity, Henry announced that the long-awaited exodus back to Africa was about to take place. Indeed, he promised, preparations were already underway and boats and planes were being sent to fetch the faithful on 5 October 1959. Thousands dutifully turned up in Kingston on the appointed day, ready to be repatriated. They were disappointed. No ships. No planes. Nothing. Henry was arrested and escaped with a small fine.

But Henry was soon back in the dock again after lawmen investigating rumours of an armed insurrection busted him with a sizeable cache of arms, explosives and a consignment of conch shells stuffed with marijuana. Henry was charged with treason and gaoled for six years.

Shortly after Henry's incarceration, his son Ronald was discovered to be leading an armed band of guerrilla rastas in the mountains. A shoot-out claimed the lives of two British soldiers, but Ronald and four of his men were eventually captured, tried and executed.

After this turbulent early history, a period of relative calm for the rastas followed, coinciding with the declaration of Jamaican independence in 1962. The following year a delegation of rastas flew to Addis Ababa for an audience with their beloved Haile Selassie. Before being admitted,

they were advised by an archbishop not to mention to the Emperor their deification of his person as it was likely to offend his sensibilities as a devout practising Christian. The visiting rastas politely heeded this advice but their faith in his divinity remained unshaken. Reasoning that 'he that humbleth himself shall be exalted' and applying a perfectly stoned logic, they deduced a confirmation of his divinity in his very denial of it.

Three years later, the Rastafarian movement's joy knew no bounds when, on 21 April 1966, the Emperor deigned actually to visit their island. Around 100,000 people turned up to meet his plane and about 60 of the leading rastas were invited to an official banquet in his honour. The date has since become a day of special celebration in the rasta calendar, requiring much smoking of the sacred herb.

Following the Emperor's overthrow and his death in 1975, the rastas' commitment to African repatriation has been put on the back burner but their faith in him as a living god remains rock solid.

Manley and Marley

In spite of a spirit of reform sweeping Jamaican society post-independence, the plight of the rastas in Kingston's ghettos remained pretty dire. They dubbed the grinding poverty of their living conditions 'the dungle' – a cross between dung and the jungle – and their reliance on ganga at this time may well have helped them cope with and blot out the awfulness of their circumstances. Things took a turn for the worse in 1966 when

"Excessive smoking of ganga has since become *de rigeur* at all rasta ceremonies and gatherings."

the authorities, in a bid to stamp out rising crime, sent in a fleet of bulldozers to destroy three Rastafarian communes.

What finally came to the rescue of the rastas and really put them on the world map was reggae music. Reggae propelled Rastafarianism into global consciousness. The popularity of acts like Toots and the Maytals and, above all, Bob Marley and the Wailers in the mid-1970s, transformed what had been an obscure and dispossessed ghetto cult into a mass-market commodity, winning converts from all over the world of every class, creed and colour. Suddenly, white middle-class rastas started appearing in London, Paris and New York.

Rastafarianism's political potential at home, meanwhile, was seized upon by the aspiring socialist Prime Minister Michael Manley who made a point of travelling out to Ethiopia for an audience with Haile Selassie. Manley also took to appearing on stage with Bob Marley in a bid to boost his popularity in the polls. It worked. Suddenly, Rastafarianism had become chic, a national institution, something to be proud of and cherished. And Michael Manley swept to electoral victory on the back of it in 1972.

Rastafarianism had finally escaped its Trenchtown ghetto, surfing on a wave of catchy reggae tunes and singing the praises of the cult's holy trinity: Marcus Garvey, Haile Selassie and, last but by no means least, the god-given gift of ganga.

The hippie trail

Cannabis culture changed forever with the coming of the hippies. Integral to the hippie way of life was firing up vast quantities of ganga and hashish. And any self-respecting stoner of the 1960s or 1970s had to cover at least a section of the hippie trail that wound its route around the major marijuana producing countries of the day, notably India, Nepal, Afghanistan, Pakistan, Lebanon and Morocco.

These hippies first started appearing in the early 1960s but their numbers were significantly swollen post-1968 – the year in which

Spliffs

The Beatles made their pilgrimage to India to sit at the feet of their Maharishi guru.

Typically, the hippies first made for the major cities but, after a while, the more adventurous among them started exploring remoter regions, often retracing networks of routes first pioneered by earlier potheads. And everywhere they went, the hippies sought out the best hashish and ganga they could find.

Prices in these early days were rock bottom and some of the more commercially minded counter-culturalists scented a profit opportunity. Demand for cannabis back home in Europe and America was escalating. Small-scale smuggling operations soon snowballed into bigger cartels shifting larger shipments. This sudden increase in First World demand for cannabis couldn't help but impact on Third World production techniques.

Of all the countries on the hippie trail, Afghanistan had by far the most sophisticated cannabis industry of the time. This was the Golden Age of Afghani hash when fields of *Cannabis indica* stretched for as far as the eye could see all over the country. These crops were used to produce sieved hashish of the highest quality. Traditionally, this had been hand rubbed – a time-consuming and labour-intensive method that was unable to keep up with the growing demands of the hippies and the Western export market they were supplying. Furthermore, hand rubbing is only really effective when using top-quality resin powder – that's why pot connoisseurs often prefer to buy unpressed

pollen and then hand rub their own hash.

The solution lay in slab pressing. This system allows much larger quantities to be produced, much faster and using inferior resin powder. Early presses were ad-libbed from whatever was lying around the place – lumps of stone, metal or wood. However, eventually more sophisticated hydraulic jack presses began filtering into the country from the West, along with metal sieves and water pumps to aid with crop irrigation.

These early hippie travellers, complete with their fancy Western technology, thus served as a catalyst for the modernisation of hashish production in Afghanistan.

However, the hippie invasion of Afghanistan and the sizeable smuggling operations that followed in its wake did not escape the attention of the Western authorities. The US, in particular, began exerting pressure on the Afghanis to clean up their act. A hashish factory near Kabul belonging to the Brotherhood of Eternal Love – a Californian smuggling cartel – was busted in 1971. Two years later Afghanistan accepted $47 million in US aid to crack down on drugs. Cannabis cultivation was promptly declared illegal and the entire year's crop destroyed.

The quality of Afghani hashish never quite recovered from this blow, although its Western export trade continued sporadically until the Soviet invasion of 1979.

Right: The Hippie Trail of the 1960s began and ended with a big, fat joint.

Mezz – A Viper Supreme

In his book *Reefer Madness*, Larry Ratso Sloman writes, 'The most legendary cat who ever blew horn or reefer was Milton (Mezz) Mezzrow.

'Mezzrow was a Jewish kid from Chicago who got in with the 'wrong' crowd early on, learned to blow some sax, and spent the rest of his seventy-three years obsessed with riffs and reefer.'

Before the Beat generation or even be-bop, Mezz – a close friend of Louis Armstrong and part-musician/part-vendor of what was esteemed as the 'best leaf on the street' – became the living embodiment of the link between jazz and pot in the 1930s, and also the authorities' worst nightmare. He was the prototype white kid hanging round the black clubs, and becoming the cultural portal through which the demonised weed would contaminate the minds of white America.

In his book, *Really The Blues*, published in 1946, Mezz draws a vivid picture of the 'viper' scene in Harlem in the period before the Second World War as a closed-off, well-organised, and highly relaxed subculture that flourished in the jazz clubs that had become hugely popular after the repeal of alcohol prohibition. When the nightspots closed their doors, the vipers moved on to the dozens of 'tea pads' that flourished in some splendour around the Savoy Ballroom on 141st Street and Lennox Avenue, and which, at their best, all but rivalled Le Club des Hachichins of 19th-century Paris. At the high end was Kaiser's, which sported three smoking lounges, a huge Wurlitzer jukebox and even hostesses who rolled neatly tailored joints for the patrons. Down-market, just about any hophead could turn his crib into a tea pad, just by putting out the word that in-the-know paying strangers could join him in what he would be doing anyway.

Street poetry

As a street poet, Mezz lovingly provides examples of the spontaneous rap of the period. 'Gun the snatcher on you left raise – the head mixer laid a bundle his way's, he's posing back like crime sure pays.' (He also offers a translation: 'Look at the detective on your left – the head bartender slipped him some hush money and he's swaggering around as if crime does pay.')

An ethical dealer, Mezz recounts how he turned down several overtures from the New York crime families, who wanted to finance a city-wide expansion of Mezz's business and thus bring marijuana to the Mob. He also wrote, and talked extensively, about pot in a vain attempt to counter the vicious misinformation generated by Henry Anslinger and the Federal Bureau of Narcotics. 'With my loaded horn I could take on all the fist swinging, evil things, in the world and bring them together in perfect harmony, spreading peace and joy and relaxation... leading all the sinners to glory.'

Unfortunately, peace and joy and relaxation were to be short-lived and the sinners went to jail

Above: Mezz blows his clarinet, but it was a different type of 'blow' that made him famous.

instead of glory. Between 1943 and 1950, Anslinger's Bureau launched an all-out, nationwide assault on the hopheads of jazz, leading to the closure of the tea pads and resulting in jailtime for celebrities like drummer Gene Krupa and actor Robert Mitchum.

Then, as the country plunged into a lengthy war, cannabis cultivation was again significantly scaled down. The little pollen still produced was redirected through the Khyber Pass to a string of Afghani refugee camps just across the Pakistani border where laws were lax and policing virtually non-existent. Here it was blended with pollen from other regions and pressed into slabs of what came to be known as Border Hash, again destined for the lucrative Western export market. Prices continued to increase and quality to suffer as progressively lower grades of pollen were adulterated with various kinds of sticky gum and other dubious binding agents.

The Nepalese capital of Kathmandu with its legendary hashish shops and lounges had also become a focal point for the early hippies and when Afghani pot production dried up post-1979, Nepalese Temple Balls increasingly started appearing on the Western markets.

Lebanese hash

Lebanon, meanwhile, had developed into by far the most important hashish-producing country in the Middle East. Its sophisticated sieving and pressing technology meant it had become a major supplier of Red Leb and Gold Leb to the North American and European markets in the 1970s and 1980s.

Lebanon had also traditionally supplied the Moroccan market with hashish. For, surprising as it may seem now considering the glut of Moroccan resin that was to follow, Morocco is a relatively recent player in the international hashish market. Cannabis in the form of *kif* has long been a part of Moroccan culture, probably for 700 years or more. Although strictly speaking illegal, the Moroccan government has always more or less tolerated its cultivation in the Rif Mountains. True, there has been the odd skirmish between soldiers and cannabis farmers in the area, notably in the late 1950s, but the fact that no other crop can be successfully grown at such high altitude has meant that most of the time the authorities have turned a blind eye to cannabis cultivation there.

Accounts differ as to how hashish production actually started in Morocco in the early 1960s but, again, it was probably the hippies who were the catalyst, introducing the Rif Mountain farmers to sophisticated sieving and pressing techniques. One particularly skilled early exponent of the art was a Moroccan nicknamed Akmed Hole in the Head – so called because of a distinctive scar. Akmed is said to have produced hashish of legendary quality, samples of which he would present to honoured guests in a gold pipe. Unfortunately, Akmed was subsequently busted in the early 1980s for his part in supplying an American smuggling ring. His assets were seized and he retired to Tangiers a spent force.

However, even without the aid of Akmed, the Moroccan hash industry continued to flourish as cash-strapped subsistence farmers cottoned on to its profit potential. The marijuana plantations became progressively bigger, spreading out from the craggy plateaux of the Rif Mountains to its lower foothills.

Meanwhile, things were not going so well in other parts of the hash-producing world. Government crackdowns in India and Pakistan vastly reduced Western exports, while a war in Lebanon likewise cut off supplies.

Morocco, with its newly created hashish industry, was perfectly positioned to capitalise on this by filling the gap. It continued steadily gaining global market share. By the end of the 1980s it had become the major supplier to Europe, the Middle East and North America as well as the world's largest exporter of hash.

But all good things come to an end and, as greed got the better of good husbandry, resources were stretched, corners were cut and quality came to be sacrificed for quantity. Unscrupulous farmers and cynical smugglers came to realise that, with demand outstripping supply, they could fob off their Western customers with substandard hashish. But they hadn't bargained for the revolution to come in the homegrown market…

The Brotherhood of Eternal Love

The Brotherhood of Eternal Love, a quasi-religious group of Californian hippies, warrants a well-earned footnote in the history of hashish.

Revering the Berkeley academic Timothy Leary – coiner of the famous 'turn on, tune in, drop out' motto – as its spaced-out guru, the Brotherhood is today principally remembered for championing

LSD. However, apart from its acid activities – which included the manufacture, distribution and unsuccessful attempt to spike the entire US water supply – another of the Brotherhood's lucrative sidelines was smuggling vast amounts of hashish from Afghanistan back to North America during the late 1960s and early 1970s.

Its first consignments were bought in the bazaars of Kandahar in 1968 for $20 a kilo ($9 a pound) – way over the going rate according to other Western smugglers of the time who accused the Brotherhood of failing to haggle, thereby driving up prices for everybody else.

Afghani primo

Glen Lynd was the main Brotherhood mule in those early days. Typically, he would buy a van in Germany and drive it overland to Afghanistan. There, he would pick up the gear and pack the camper's panels with enormous slabs of hashish before driving on over the Pakistan border to the port of Karachi where he would ship it back to the US. Gradually, the Brotherhood's consignments got larger and Afghani hash began flooding into the US and Canada, where it became known as Afghani Primo.

Getting wind of this, the US authorities dispatched a drug enforcement agent out to Kabul to keep an eye on things. Pressure was also put on the Afghani authorities to cooperate. The heightened policing paid off and a 320kg (700lb) consignment of Afghani Primo, again hidden in a camper van, was subsequently

Above: Timothy Leary turns on, tunes in, and drops out.

interception on arrival in Vancouver. A few months later a further 600kg (1,300lb) was seized by customs on arrival in Portland, Oregon.

Meanwhile, back in a Californian laboratory, Bobby Andrist, one of the Brotherhood's brightest sparks, was perfecting a method for producing hash oil. This is a hashish derivative in which the THC content – the principal psychoactive agent of cannabis – is refined into a honey-coloured oil. Hash oil is both stronger and more concentrated than regular hash and therefore commands a much higher price. Even back in the early 1970s it was selling for as much as $10,000 a litre ($5,500 a pint). It is also easier to conceal than regular hash.

This was all great news for the smugglers. So, the next step was for the Brotherhood to set up a string of hash oil laboratories in Afghanistan under the supervision of Andrist. All went well for the first few months until an explosion in one of the laboratories near Kabul in 1971 alerted the authorities as to what was going on.

Andrist and a number of his accomplices were busted and wound up facing criminal charges in California in 1972. The Brotherhood's hashish-smuggling heyday was over.

Sensi to the rescue

By the early 1970s the trade in smuggled cannabis was becoming increasingly fraught and problematic. The greed endemic in the supply chain – from the farmers through to the smugglers and the dealers – was becoming unsustainable. Prices were rocketing while quality was plummeting.

Moreover, the US authorities were becoming increasingly vigilant and efficient in busting smugglers and in destroying crops. By 1969 the war against the weed had become so systematic that President Nixon had ordered Mexican marijuana crops to be sprayed from the air with paraquat – a highly toxic chemical that can cause lung diseases.

North American smokers retaliated the only way they could – they started growing their own. And within a short space of time they proved themselves very good at it. Home growing had first started in the early 1960s but back then it had been very much a hit-and-miss affair with yields of random size and quality.

Then, in the mid-1970s, everything changed. The cannabis chronicler Robert Connell Clarke

pinpoints the 1976 publication of the seminal *Sensimilla Marijuana Flowers* by Jim Richardson and Arik Woods as being the turning point. The coming of sensimilla was totally to change the face of cannabis culture.

Weeding out useless males

The word sensimilla derives from the Spanish, meaning literally 'without seed'. As cannabis plants develop, both the male and female plants produce distinct flowers. However, the psychoactive THC compound, so beloved of potheads, is only to be found in the female flowers. To obtain a crop of sensi it is necessary to weed out the useless male plants early on in the growing cycle, before they release the pollen which makes the females go to seed. Once the males are out, the females undergo a kind of false pregnancy, producing seedless blossoms prolifically in a bid to attract the absent males. When peak florescence is reached, the plants are harvested, manicured and dried. The result is sweet-tasting sensimilla.

Prior to this, all marijuana had been seeded, even the types used in the manufacture of top-grade hashish. Sensimilla was thus a whole new departure, invented by American tokers of the 1970s who had become fed up with the quality of imported marijuana and hashish. Its discovery and development was to have a profound effect in more ways than one.

The seeds used by the early American growers were mainly sourced from batches of imported marijuana from Latin America, the Caribbean and Thailand. Early experiments in cultivation were haphazard – some strains responded well to the new climates and conditions, others not so well. However, all of these early varieties were *Cannabis sativa* – resulting in tall bushy plants with good flavour and high levels of potency. They were cultivated outdoors where, under the right conditions, each plant could grow to more than 8ft (2.5m) tall and produce several kilos of fine bud – representing an extremely profitable cash crop.

However, high visibility has its problems, especially with the DEA and FBI sending out regular reconnaissance flights over the remoter regions of California and Washington where the cultivation was most prevalent. Thieves, too, were a problem for the early growers who could hardly complain to the police if their crops were stolen.

Then, in the late 1970s, US breeders got hold of some *Cannabis indica* seeds from Afghanistan and Pakistan. Indica is the yin to sativa's yang. While sativa is big and bushy, indica is compact and chunky. Although opinion is divided as to which type is actually the best smoke, the appearance of *Cannabis indica* on the scene and the controlled cross-breeding programme that followed significantly helped the growers. Outdoor crops of four-foot plants suddenly became possible. Indica also matures quicker than sativa. This meant earlier harvests with less likelihood of crop detection.

Hydroponics create indoor boom

Another bonus of the arrival of indica was that it opened up the way for indoor cultivation where space is so often at a premium. Suddenly small-scale indoor growers were able to produce three to four harvests a year with each dwarf plant yielding up to three to four ounces (around 100g) of top bud.

Hydroponic systems proved particularly popular among indoor cultivators. Such systems use alternative growing mediums to soil such as Rockwool – a neutral spongy medium normally used for loft insulation. Diluted nutrients are pumped through the Rockwool from a mini-reservoir beneath the growing platform. Hydroponic systems can be made fully automatic and hassle free by deploying timer-operated lights and pumps. By regulating lighting regimes, patterns of plant growth can be tightly controlled too.

A whole new generation of closet growers thus came into being. Borrowing and adapting from existing horticultural technology, fully mechanised mini drug factories started whirring into action in the spare rooms, wardrobes and cupboards of potheads all over America.

Cannabis-breeding programmes also became increasingly sophisticated with specific strains being developed for indoor and outdoor cultivation. Networks of breeders began pooling their seeds, which were sourced from ever remoter regions around the world. Gene banks were set up and scrupulously detailed records kept to aid the breeders in developing new

Above: Hydroponically-grown sensimilla.
Right: Commercially available Sensi seeds.

hybrid strains. Cuttings could be taken from
established male and female plants and then
interbred over many generations to develop new
hybrid types of known ancestry.

Over the next ten years many hybrid types of
high-grade marijuana were developed. Such was
the speed at which this remarkable growing
programme developed that by the early 1980s US
marijuana was universally acknowledged to be the
best in the world. Old 1970s 'brands' like Acapulco
Gold, Durban Poison and Thai Sticks were a thing
of the past, their thunder stolen by homegrown

"all of these early varieties were cannabis sativa – resulting in tall bushy plants"

newcomers like Skunk, Hindu Kush and Haze.

The identity of these pioneering US breeders remains a mystery – they were, after all, operating outside of the law. However, they were undoubtedly horticulturalists of the highest calibre. They brought a scientific exactitude and discipline to the art of cannabis cultivation it had previously lacked and – through the shadowy Sacred Seed Company, which they set up in California on a need-to-know basis – bequeathed us many of the best sensimilla strains still being smoked around the world to this day.

Marijuana mecca

Since the early 1980s the science of sensi has moved to the more liberal soil of Amsterdam in the Netherlands. Amsterdam was the obvious choice to act as European gateway for the new growing techniques as it was already home to a thriving cannabis culture. Imported hash or grass could be scored openly across the counter in any one of its hundreds of licensed coffee shops where printed menus often listed more than two dozen varieties.

However, up until the arrival of sensi in the early 1980s, all the cannabis in Amsterdam was imported. The locals had tried their hand at growing their own but the results had been largely disappointing. Nevertheless, once equipped with the technical know-how and a few batches of cuttings supplied by the Sacred Seed Company, there was no holding the Dutch back.

Euro hybrids

Within a few years, half a dozen reputable seed companies had appeared and the air of Amsterdam's coffee shops had become thick with the smoke of such early American classics as Haze, Hindu Kush, Big Bud and Northern Lights.

The Dutch initiated their own breeding programmes, too, sourcing seeds from Asia and the Middle East to develop new generations of hybrids such as Holland's Hope and Amstel Gold, to name but two.

Amsterdam also acted as the catalyst in turning on the rest of Europe to the science of sensimilla, supplying seeds and equipment to the pioneering homegrowers of Great Britain, Germany, Austria and Switzerland.

Right: One of Amsterdam's 300-plus licensed coffee shops.

A Bad Case of Medicinal Marijuana

After two years of doctor-and-patient testimony, the Drug Enforcement Agency's chief administrative law judge, Francis L. Young, ruled that 'marijuana in its natural form is one of the safest therapeutically active substances known to man'.

He went on to condemn its prohibition as 'unreasonable, arbitrary and capricious', and he ordered the DEA to re-categorise pot so it could be available on prescription. With this judgement, Young opened one of the most bizarre and indefensible chapters in the war on drugs, and one that would clearly demonstrate that the marijuana opposition are determined that the herb remain illegal, no matter how absurd their case becomes.

For years, anecdotal evidence had circulated as to how reefer was effective in the treatment of an array of illnesses, including glaucoma, anorexia, chronic pain, arthritis, and migraine. It demonstrably mitigated the vomiting caused by chemotherapy, and the attendant munchies could restore the appetite of AIDS sufferers in the tissue-wasting phase of the disease – known as the 'Auschwitz effect'. On this evidence alone, logic seemed to dictate that to make pot available on prescription was an act of both compassion and common sense – but the Federal Government thought otherwise.

No smoke for the sick

DEA Director Jack Lawn sat on Judge Young's decision for 15 months and then overturned it, presumably thinking that that had ended the medical marijuana debate for the time being. What Lawn and subsequent DEA directors failed to appreciate was the tenacity of the gay community who, observing that medical marijuana was an actual life-saver for some AIDS patients, and having already spent a decade fighting for government recognition of the entire AIDS crisis, were not about to accept the DEA's decision passively. The fight was taken to the state level, where the California Legislature passed a bill – three times – that legalised the medicinal use of cannabis, only to have all three bills vetoed by Governor Pete Wilson for no better reason than, 'It sends the wrong message to our kids.'

In the election of 1996, Arizona and California – states in which voters not only elect their state representatives, but also pass numbered propositions – the legalisation of medical marijuana was on the ballot as Proposition 200, and 215 respectively. Both passed, by 57 per cent in California and a massive 65 per cent in Arizona.

Now the people had spoken and that, surely, had to be an end to it. Not so, decided the DEA and the Justice Department, declaring that there

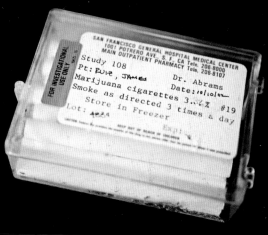

Above: Medically-prescribed marijuana.

wasn't 'a shred of evidence' for marijuana's therapeutic value, and also that Props 200 and 215 were 'a Trojan Horse' for full decriminalisation. To prove their point, cannabis clubs supplying pot to the sick were closed and the organisers were arrested and charged. Doctors who prescribed the drug were threatened, and even nursing homes and hospices for the dying were raided. When George Bush replaced Bill Clinton, the policy was not only maintained but stepped up, under Attorney General John Ashcroft. Even in the wake of the 9/11 disaster, the raids and arrests continue, with no sign of even a compromise in sight.

"Cannabis is not strictly speaking legal in the Netherlands... "

Amsterdam today is a marijuana mecca, attracting enthusiasts from all over the world and annually hosting the Cannabis Cup – a pot fest organised by the American magazine *High Times*. The city boasts more than a dozen seed dealers offering more than 150 different seed varieties.

The trade in sensimilla is now booming, not only in Amsterdam but also worldwide.

Legalise it

Considering the prevalence of pot in Amsterdam, it is surely an anomaly that cannabis is not strictly speaking legal in the Netherlands. In fact, the sale of marijuana is technically illegal, despite the fact that the coffee shop trade is in practice tolerated and even licensed. Possession of up to 5g (a little over ⅙oz) by the punter and up to 50g (1¾oz) by the retailer does not attract prosecution.

This state of legal limbo is known as decriminalisation. And though decriminalisation is better than outright prohibition, the flip side to it is that the people supplying the coffee shops are still operating outside of the law and face serious criminal charges if caught.

There is really only one way to eradicate such inconsistencies: unequivocal legalisation.

The good news is that greater tolerance towards cannabis seems to be spreading across Europe. The Belgians have legalised the possession, cultivation and importation of 'reasonable' amounts for personal use, while Luxembourg recently implemented decriminalisation. Switzerland is in the process of following suit. Meanwhile, other European countries are becoming increasingly lax in their enforcement of the law. Small amounts are usually overlooked in Sweden, Norway, Italy, Spain, Portugal, Germany, Denmark and Ireland. In Britain, too, although the government remains opposed to legalisation, enforcement has become noticeably less stringent with cannabis commerce now more or less tolerated in certain areas of London.

That is not to say that all Europeans are proving equally enlightened. Draconian Greek and Finnish laws are still being enforced savagely, while French legislation fails even to distinguish between soft and hard drugs.

Better news comes from across the Atlantic in Canada, which recently lifted its ban on using cannabis medicinally. Canadian attitudes towards its recreational use also appear to be relaxing, with a recent government committee reporting, 'Scientific evidence overwhelmingly indicates that cannabis is substantially less harmful than

alcohol and should be treated not as a criminal issue but as a social and public health issue.'

Unfortunately, the picture is not quite so encouraging across the border in the United States. Although there are pockets of progress – possession of small amounts has been decriminalised in New York, Alaska and California – there are still far too many people going to gaol. The National Organization for the

Above: Amsterdam's coffee shops are a smoker's sanctuary... the ideal place to skin-up, kick back and chill.

Reform of Marijuana Laws (NORML) estimates that almost six million Americans have been busted for spliff since 1990, nearly 750,000 of them in 2000 alone. That's one bust every 45 seconds. Enough already.

Chapter 2

Top Draw

"Dope will get you through times of no money better than money will get you through times of no dope" The Fabulous Furry Freak Brothers

Top Draw

Our spotter's guide features the best grass and hash on the planet.

🌿 **MILD**

🌿🌿 **MEDIUM**

🌿🌿🌿 **STRONG**

🌿🌿🌿🌿 **VERY STRONG**

🌿🌿🌿🌿🌿 **HUH?**

What are the relative merits of grass versus hash? If one were to judge it purely by the strength of the smoke, then hash is the clear winner. This is because, in its purest state, hash contains significantly more THC – the chief psychoactive ingredient of cannabis – than grass. However, just as judging fine wines by alcohol content would be patently absurd, so too is the attempt to grade cannabis solely by its potency. There is no definitive league table when it comes to cannabis. Value judgements do not really apply and one type of hash or grass cannot really be said to be any 'better' or 'worse' than any another. In the final analysis it just boils down to personal taste.

Aesthetic factors, such as flavour and appearance, play a role, as does etiquette and the social setting. One of the main factors to be borne in mind is that hash highs are generally heavier and more soporific than grass ones. Grass tends to produce a mellower and more cerebral high. That means that hashish is often more suitable for those quiet nights in, while ganga comes into its own more on more sociable occasions.

The following selection of grass and hash types is by no means exhaustive. Indeed, recent developments in cannabis culture – notably the sensimilla revolution and the development of domestically produced Nederhash in Holland – rules out that possibility. That is because there are now literally hundreds of different marijuana strains out there and scope for the future development of new strains seems virtually infinite. And as we now have the technology in place to produce a different type of hash for every different type of sensimilla, any attempt to produce a definitive guide is doomed to failure before it even begins.

Research is further hindered by the air of secrecy surrounding the subject and the fact that different strains often acquire different names in different places.

Bearing all these difficulties in mind, however, the following selection of grass (listed alphabetically) and hash (listed geographically) types provides at least a rough idea of the vast variety of cannabis that is currently on offer.

Drool on, dudes.

Grass

"... to be peaceful without being stupid, to be interested without being compulsive, to be happy without being hysterical ... smoke grass."

Ken Kesey

AK-47

THIS LITTLE LADY IS A SERIOUS SMOKE. A HYBRID MIX OF THE BEST IN INDICA AND SATIVA, SHE'S WON MORE CANNABIS AWARDS THAN YOU COULD SHAKE A STICK AT. AK-47 DELIVERS A SMOOTH BUT PUNGENT SMOKE. THE HIGH IS NON-DEBILITATING AND THE FLAVOUR IS STRONG WITH HINTS OF DAMSON AND CITRUS. YOU'LL ENJOY THE RIDE.

BLUEBERRY

BLUEBERRY IS OOZING WITH FRUITY FLAVOURS – AS ONE WOULD EXPECT FROM A STRAIN THAT FEATURES JUICY FRUIT THAI IN ITS PEDIGREE. BRED BY THE DISTINGUISHED HORTICULTURALIST DJ SHORT, HE ALSO USED AFGHANI INDICA AND PURPLE THAI TO GET THE BALANCE JUST RIGHT. A CANNABIS CUP WINNER IN 2000, THIS ONE IS GUARANTEED TO KEEP YOU ON YOUR TOES.

BUBBLEGUM

A CURIOUS AMERICAN INDICA STRAIN FROM INDIANA THAT ARRIVED IN AMSTERDAM ABOUT 10 YEARS AGO. APTLY NAMED – IT ACTUALLY TASTES SACCHARINE AND PINK – ITS GLANDS AND FLOWERS DELIVER A EUPHORIC HIGH THAT LASTS FOR HOURS. IT WAS BRED BY CROSSING NORTHERN LIGHTS 5 WITH BIG SKUNK.

CRYSTAL

CRYSTAL MAY WELL BE SO NAMED BECAUSE OF THE CLARITY OF THE HIGH IT DELIVERS. IT HAS A CLEAN FLAVOUR TOO AND GOES DOWN EASY WITHOUT CLOGGING THE THROAT. YET THERE IS A SWEET PUNGENCY THERE TOO, HINTING AT A SATIVA HERITAGE. CRYSTAL IS A GOOD RELIABLE TOKE FOR THOSE OCCASIONS WHEN YOU WANT TO KEEP A CLEAR MIND AND A STEADY HAND.

EDELWEISS

THE EDELWEISS STRAIN WAS
DEVELOPED IN HOLLAND FROM
INDICA PARENTS. IT HAS A STRONG
SPICY FLAVOUR AND A FULL TASTE.
SMOKE IT TO ACHIEVE A MELLOW
AND MASTERFUL HIGH. IT WILL GET
YOU FULL-ON STONED WITHOUT
BLOWING YOUR BRAINS OUT.
RECOMMENDED TO SMOKE
SOCIALLY AS IT MAKES PARTIES GO
WITH A SWING.

HEAVEN'S HAZE

THIS HYBRID IS A REAL STAR,
COMBINING THE BEST FEATURES OF
FOUR DIFFERENT SATIVAS SOURCED
FROM ALL OVER THE WORLD:
THAILAND, MEXICO, COLOMBIA AND
INDIA. THE RESULT IS A SUPER-
STRONG HIGH THAT WILL KEEP YOU
ZINGING FOR HOURS. THE FLAVOUR
WILL KNOCK YOU OUT TOO – SWEET
WITHOUT BEING CLOYING AND WITH
A SPICY PEPPER EDGE. THIS IS ONE
THAT HAS TO BE SMOKED TO BE
BELIEVED.

HIMALAYA
🍁 🍁 🍁

ANOTHER DUTCH CHAMPION, THIS INDICA-BASED SENSI HAS A UNIQUE SPICY LEMON FLAVOUR. A LOT OF WORK HAS GONE INTO ITS BREEDING AND STABILIZATION. IT LEAVES A DELIGHTFUL NOTE OF CITRUS ON THE TASTE BUDS AND IS VERY, VERY STRONG. AFTER LIGHTING THE TOUCH PAPER, TREAT WITH EXTREME CAUTION. AND ALLOW YOURSELF A FEW HOURS TO RETURN TO PLANET EARTH.

JACK HERER
🍁 🍁 🍁 🍁 🍁

NAMED AFTER THE CANNABIS ACTIVIST AND AUTHOR OF *THE EMPEROR WEARS NO CLOTHES*, THIS IS A MULTIPLE HYBRID COMBINING THREE OF THE STRONGEST VARIETIES KNOWN TO MANKIND. FRUITY AND SPICY, IT IS ONE OF THE MORE POPULAR STRAINS FROM AMSTERDAM'S SENSI SEED BANK. THE FLOWERS BRISTLE WITH RESIN GLANDS AND THE EFFECT IS CEREBRAL AND MORE OR LESS INSTANTANEOUS. ONLY FOR THE INTREPID.

K2

☘ ☘

NAMED AFTER THE HIMALAYAN
MOUNTAIN NESTLING IN THE
SHADOW OF EVEREST, K2 IS A
MULTIPLE CROSS OF STRAINS
INCLUDING NORTHERN LIGHTS 2,
HAZE, KUSH AND EARLY PEARL. AS A
RESULT IT IS SOMEWHAT LACKING
IN PERSONALITY. ALTHOUGH IT HAS
A REASONABLE KICK TO IT, SOME
SMOKERS FIND IT BLAND AND ARE
PUT OFF BY ITS CHEESY FLAVOUR.
JUDGE FOR YOURSELF.

KAHUNA

☘ ☘ ☘

AN INDICA OOZING WITH MANGO
RESIN. ITS SMOKE IS DENSE AND
LUSCIOUS AND ITS EFFECT
SOOTHING. SOMEHOW ALL THOSE
TROUBLES SEEM TO SLIP AWAY AS
YOU SIT BACK AND PUFF
CONTENTEDLY ON THIS JUICY WEED.
BANISH YOUR ANXIETY AND
ENVELOPE YOURSELF IN A
LUXURIOUS DUVET OF WELLBEING.

KALI MIST

🌿 🌿 🌿 🌿

THIS IS A WICKED SATIVA. IT MAY BE HARD TO GROW BUT IT WILL REPAY YOUR PATIENCE. AS A RESULT IT TENDS TO BE LESS GROWN FOR COMMERCIAL PURPOSES, MORE FOR PERSONAL STASHES. ITS PARENTAGE IS SLIGHTLY QUESTIONABLE BUT MOST EXPERTS AGREE THAT THERE IS A LOT OF HAZE IN THERE. IT DELIVERS A FLAVOUR AND HIGH TO DIE FOR.

ORANGE BUD

🌿

RATHER DISAPPOINTING SKUNK HYBRID PRODUCED IN AMSTERDAM WHICH LEAVES ONE FEELING STRANGELY FLAT AND BEWILDERED. ITS SATIVA SWEETNESS IS A LITTLE CLOYING. WITH THE EXCEPTION OF THE CHAMPION SKUNK 1, MOST OF THE SKUNK HYBRIDS HAVE NOT TRANSLATED WELL TO DUTCH SOIL. ONE OF THOSE EXPERIMENTS THAT WENT SLIGHTLY WRONG.

POWERPLANT
🍁 🍁 🍁 🍁

POWERPLANT IS A GOOD EXAMPLE OF A POTENT SOUTH AFRICAN SATIVA WITH ALL THE JUICY SWEETNESS OF A TOP-NOTCH HAWAIIAN. IT SMOKES EASILY, NOT CATCHING THE BACK OF THE THROAT AND PRODUCES A SILKY [???]. THE HIGH CAN BE TALL ON THIS ONE BUT WITH TIME IT MELLOWS OUT INTO A PEACHY SMOOTH DAYDREAM.

PUNTA-ROSA
🍁 🍁 🍁

THIS LOVELY LADY BLOSSOMS BEST OUTDOORS. IF YOU'VE GOT THE SPACE, PUNTA ROSA IS EASY TO GROW AND CONSISTENTLY DELIVERS BUMPER HARVESTS. A HYBRID SATIVA ORIGINALLY FROM MEXICO, THE PLANT HAS A SWEET AND SPICY FLAVOUR AND DELIVERS A PROLONGED BUT MANAGEABLE HIGH. JUST SKIN UP, TAKE A LONG TOKE AND DREAM YOURSELF OFF TO ACAPULCO.

ROCK BUD

🌿 🌿 🌿

A CANNABIS CUP WINNER IN 1998, ROCK BUD IS A RELIABLE DUTCH INDICA DELIVERING A FRESH SWEET SMOKE. IT BLENDS SUBTLE FRUIT FLAVOURS OF STRAWBERRY, BANANA AND LEMON. DON'T BE FOOLED THOUGH. IT'S GOT A KICK LIKE A MULE AND CHANCES ARE YOU'LL BE LYING FLAT ON YOUR BACK TEN MINUTES LATER. BEST RESERVED FOR THOSE QUIET NIGHTS IN.

SAGE

🌿 🌿 🌿 🌿 🌿

SAGE, STANDING FOR SATIVA AFGHANI GENETIC EQUILIBRIUM, IS THE RESULT OF CROSSING A SATIVA HAZE WITH A STRONG INDICA. ITS HIGH THC CONTENT – 20 PER CENT – AND POLISHED SANDALWOOD FLAVOUR MADE IT A CLEAR WINNER AT THE 2000 CANNABIS CUP. RUMOURED TO HAVE SOME OF THE LEGENDARY AMERICAN BIG SUR HOLY WEED IN ITS GENETIC BACKGROUND. HEAVEN BE PRAISED!

SALAD BOWL

A COCKTAIL SERVED UP AT
AMSTERDAM'S LEGENDARY
DAMPKRING COFFEE SHOP. THIS IS
THE STUFF THAT'S LEFT OVER WHEN
THE BIG BUDS HAVE BEEN SOLD – A
GUMBO THROWN TOGETHER FROM
ALL THE LEFTOVERS. NOT EXACTLY
SAWDUST BUT ITS QUALITY CAN BE
VARIABLE. CHEAP AND CHEERFUL.

SANTA MARIA

YET ANOTHER DUTCH INDICA WHOSE
FANS SMOKE IT RELIGIOUSLY. AN
INDOOR PLANT, IT HAS A PUNGENT,
SLIGHTLY ACRID AROMA BUT
SMOKES SMOOTHLY AND CARRIES
WITH IT A STRONG, SPICY
AFTERTASTE. NOT FOR THE
FAINTHEARTED, IT'S MORE SITTING-
DOWN STONED THAN LOOKING
LIVELY. A GOOD ONE TO UNWIND
WITH AFTER WORK.

SILVER HAZE

🍁 🍁 🍁 🍁

SOME REGARD THIS STRAIN AS THE APOTHEOSIS OF CANNABIS CULTIVATION. IT POSITIVELY DRIPS WITH RESIN GLANDS AND ITS ILLUSTRIOUS FOREBEARS INCLUDE SUCH OLD ARISTOS AS NORTHERN LIGHTS 5, HAZE AND SKUNK 1. THEY DON'T COME MUCH CLASSIER THAN THIS. THE FLAVOUR AND POTENCY CAN SOMETIMES PROVE A LITTLE OVERWHELMING, BUT YOU'RE DUTY BOUND TO FILL YOUR BOOTS.

STELLA BLUE

🍁 🍁 🍁

ONE OF THOSE RARE DUTCH SATIVAS THAT LIVE UP TO THEIR REPUTATION. STELLA BLUE IS STRONG ON FRUIT FLAVOURS WITH JUST A HINT OF ANISEED. A CANNABIS CUP PRIZE WINNER IN 1995, STELLA BLUE HAS SINCE GONE THE DISTANCE AND ESTABLISHED ITSELF AS A FIRM FAVOURITE IN MANY OF AMSTERDAM'S MOST DISCERNING COFFEE SHOPS. ONE FOR THE CONNOISSEUR.

SUPER CITRAL

AN UNUSUAL DUTCH INDICA WITH SPICY CITRUS NOTES AND A STRONG HIGH. THE BUDS BRISTLE WITH RESIN GLANDS AND THE EFFECT OF SMOKING IT IS INSTANTANEOUS. HOWEVER, THE HIGH CAN BE TOO NARCOTIC, LEADING TO PARANOIA AND WOBBLY KNEES. DOES NOT MIX WELL WITH ALCOHOL AND SHOULD ONLY BE SMOKED IN MODERATION AND LATE AT NIGHT.

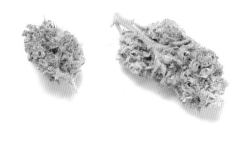

SUPER THAI

STANDARD OUTDOOR VARIETY FOR EVERYDAY SMOKING. IT HAS A PLEASANT SPICY FLAVOUR AND HELPS LIFT THE SPIRITS WITHOUT IMPAIRING PERFORMANCE. THERE MIGHT BE BETTER STRAINS OUT THERE, BUT FEW ARE MORE RELIABLE. ONE MINOR DRAWBACK OF THE SUPER THAI IS THAT IT IS A DEAD GIVEAWAY – YOUR EYES GO BLOODSHOT.

THAI

ROCK BOTTOM OF THE OUTDOOR RANGE BUT NOT WITHOUT ITS MERITS. IT DIFFERS FROM SUPER THAI IN BEING A LITTLE LESS POTENT AND HAVING A SLIGHTLY SOURER FLAVOUR. THE HIGH IS HARSHER TOO BUT THERE IS NO ARGUING WITH ITS GREAT VALUE FOR MONEY. THAI WILL HELP YOU THROUGH THE HARD TIMES AND THROW IN A FEW GIGGLES TO EASE YOUR WEARY WAY.

TOP 44

GOT ITS NAME FROM THE FACT THAT FEMALE PLANTS ARE FULLY MATURE AND READY FOR HARVEST WITHIN 44 DAYS. TOP 44 IS DUTCH BRED AND MAINLY INDICA. IT HAS A FULL FRUITY FLAVOUR AND SMOKES NICELY. HOWEVER THE HIGH TENDS TO BE SHALLOW AND SHORT LIVED. MIGHT MAKE SENSE FOR CASH-STRAPPED GROWERS BUT NOT A GREAT CHOICE FOR THE SMOKERS. WILL ONLY REALLY DO FOR WANT OF BETTER.

WARLOCK HAZE
🌿 🌿 🌿 🌿

ANOTHER WINNER FROM THE FABULOUS HAZE STABLE. A DUTCH SATIVA, IT NEVERTHELESS HAS A SWEET SPICY AROMA. ITS FLOWERS ARE RESIN-PACKED BUT THE SMOKE DRAWS EASILY. SCRAMBLES BRAINS AND BRINGS ON FITS OF GIGGLING. ITS WARLOCK SIDE IS RELATED TO SKUNK 1 AND THE CHEMISTRY BETWEEN THE TWO HAS CLEARLY WORKED MAGIC. WARLOCK HAZE IS ONE TO WATCH.

WHITE RUSSIAN
🌿 🌿 🌿

WHITE RUSSIAN IS A CROSS BETWEEN AK-47 AND WHITE WIDOW. IT HAS A STRONG CITRUS-TO-MANGO FLAVOUR AND ITS BUDS ARE OFTEN PLUMP, JUICY AND COVERED WITH A FINE LAYER OF STICKY GLANDS. STRAINS WITH FROSTED LEAVES AND FLOWERS LIKE THIS ARE COMPARATIVELY RARE. THE HIGH PROVIDES A STRONG LIFT BUT SMOKING TOO MUCH AT ONE GO CAN BE HARD ON THE THROAT.

WHITE WIDOW
🍁 🍁 🍁 🍁

WHITE WIDOW IS AN INDICA AND SATIVA HYBRID PRODUCED BY CROSSING AN INDIAN AND BRAZILIAN STRAIN. ITS BOUQUET BLENDS HERBAL AROMAS WITH A CITRUS DIRECTNESS AND THE HIGH IT PRODUCES IS DEEP, LEADING TO THE LAND OF DREAMY DREAMS. ITS SMOKE IS DENSE AND CHESTY AND ITS EFFECTS TEND TO PERSIST FOR A GOOD COUPLE OF HOURS.

YUMBOLDT
🍁 🍁 🍁 🍁

ORIGINALLY NAMED AFTER HUMBOLDT COUNTY IN CALIFORNIA WHICH IS HOME TO SOME OF THE BEST WEED IN THE WORLD. THIS BATCH WAS RAISED OUTDOORS FROM SATIVA AND INDICA HYBRIDS. IT HAS A CREAMY, MELONY FLAVOUR AND A STRONG CEREBRAL HIGH. A LITTLE GOES A LONG WAY AND IT IS BEST SAVED FOR SPECIAL OCCASIONS – AFTER DESSERT PREFERABLY. THIS IS ONE TO REALLY SAVOUR.

79

Hash

"Hashish spreads itself over all life; as it were, the magic varnish. It colours it with solemn hues and lights up all its profundity."

Charles Baudelaire, *'The Poem of Hashish'*

AFGHANI BLACK
[AFGHANISTAN]
🍁 🍁 🍁 🍁

TOP-GRADE HASH FROM AFGHANISTAN IS BECOMING INCREASINGLY RARE. THIS PIECE HAS BEEN HYDRAULICALLY PRESSED AND HAS THE SIGNATURE PEPPERY FLAVOUR OF THE GENUINE ARTICLE – THE FLAVOUR IS ENHANCED THE LONGER IT IS PRESSED. THE SMOKE IS BILLOWING AND WHITE AND THE HIGH IS DEBILITATING. DON'T PLAN ON GETTING MUCH DONE AFTER A SPLIFF OR TWO OF THIS.

AFGHANI POLLEN
[AFGHANISTAN]
🍁 🍁

SKIN UP ONE OF THESE NUMBERS AND FORGET YOUR TROUBLES. BRIEFLY PRESSED AFGHANI POLLEN PRODUCES A SLIGHTLY LIGHTER AND CRUMBLIER HASH THAN TRADITIONAL AFGHANI BLACK. THE HIGH IS A LOT MELLOWER, TOO, AND THE SMOKE LESS HARSH. BUT WHAT YOU GAIN ON THE SWINGS YOU LOSE ON THE ROUNDABOUTS – THE FLAVOUR IS LESS ROUNDED AND DEVELOPED.

INDIAN HAND-RUBBED
[INDIA]

🌿 🌿 🌿

HAND-RUBBED HASH FROM
HIMACHEL PRADESH STATE IN
NORTHERN INDIA – A TRADITION
GOING BACK MANY THOUSANDS OF
YEARS. BEST SMOKED IN A CHILLUM,
THIS SPICY CHARAS WILL PUT A
SMILE ON YOUR FACE IN NO TIME.
BEWARE, THOUGH, THIS IS NO MILD
MOROCCAN BUZZ – BUDGET FOR
BEING OFF YOUR FACE FOR QUITE A
FEW HOURS.

MELANA CREAM
[INDIA]

🌿 🌿 🌿 🌿 🌿

DON'T BE FOOLED BY ITS SWEET
FLORAL BOUQUET AND INNOCENT
BEGUILING FLAVOUR – THIS ONE
PACKS A PUNCH. MELANA COMES
FROM THE KULU VALLEY IN
HIMACHEL PRADESH AND WAS SEEN
A LOT IN THE WEST IN THE 1970s AND
1980s. IT CONTINUES TO BE HAND-
RUBBED IN THE TRADITIONAL WAY
BUT NOWADAYS IT'S RARELY SEEN
OUTSIDE ITS NATIVE INDIA.

CREAM
[INDIA]
❋ ❋ ❋ ❋
ANOTHER KNOCK-OUT HASH FROM NORTHERN INDIA. THE PARVATTI VALLEY PRODUCES SOME OF THE BEST HASH ON THE INDIAN SUBCONTINENT AND CREAM IS, WELL… THE CRÈME DE LA CRÈME. THE FLAVOUR IS A SUBTLE BLEND OF CARDAMOM AND MANGO WHILE THE HIGH TRANSPORTS YOU TO A TRULY HIGHER LEVEL OF BEING. ONE TO TELL YOUR GRANDCHILDREN ABOUT.

GOLD LEBANESE
[LEBANON]
❋ ❋ ❋
ONCE A FAMILIAR SIGHT IN THE WEST, GOLD LEB IS NOW RARELY SEEN OTHER THAN IN THE MORE SOPHISTICATED OF AMSTERDAM'S COFFEE SHOPS. BUT IT IS A FINE SMOKE STILL – RUBBERY AND CRUMBLY IN CONSISTENCY, ROUNDED AND GENEROUS IN FLAVOUR. SMOKES WELL IN COMPANY, STIMULATING A FRIENDLY GLOW AND A SOCIABLE BUZZ. PUT IT IN YOUR PIPE AND PASS IT ROUND.

NEPALESE
[NEPAL]

FROM HIGH UP IN THE HIMALAYAS IN
THE MOUNTAIN KINGDOM OF NEPAL.
A LITTLE NUGGET LIKE THIS CAN BE
SCORED ON THE STREETS OF
KATHMANDU FOR NEXT TO NOTHING.
NEPALESE HAS A RICH CHOCOLATEY
FLAVOUR AND CAN SERIOUSLY MESS
WITH YOUR MIND IF SMOKED IN
SUFFICIENT QUANTITIES.

ROYAL NEPALESE
[NEPAL]

A HASH TO BE TREATED WITH
RESPECT. THE CANNABIS SCHOLAR
LAURENCE CHERNIAC WROTE BACK IN
1979, 'ONE DEEP PUFF OF FIRST
QUALITY ROYAL NEPALI HASHISH
MAKES YOU FEEL BODILESS YET
SUPER-SENSUAL.' THOSE WORDS
HOLD EQUALLY TRUE TODAY. ROYAL
NEPALI OPENS UP A PARALLEL
UNIVERSE. ONCE SMOKED, NEVER
FORGOTTEN. ONE OF THE REAL
CANNABIS KINGS.

NEPALESE TEMPLE BALLS
[NEPAL]
✹ ✹ ✹ ✹ ✹

ANOTHER FIRST-CLASS SMOKE FROM THE KINGDOM IN THE CLOUDS. THE LEGENDARY NEPALESE TEMPLE BALLS REALLY DID ORIGINATE IN THE BUDDHIST TEMPLES OF NEPAL WHERE THEY CONTINUE TO BE USED RITUALISTICALLY. THEY ARE HAND-RUBBED INTO SPHERICAL EGGS, BLACK AND SHINY ON THE OUTSIDE AND A RICH EARTHY BROWN WITHIN. WHEN SMOKED THEY LET OFF A PATCHOULI FRAGRANCE AND THEIR DEPTH OF FLAVOUR MATCHES THAT OF ANY VINTAGE WINE.

CARAMELLO
[MOROCCO]
✹ ✹ ✹

CARAMELLO IS THE SPANISH SLANG FOR THIS TYPE OF MOROCCAN POT FROM THE FOOTHILLS OF THE RIF MOUNTAINS. THIS PIECE IS TYPICAL OF THE HASH THAT YOU ARE LIKELY TO FIND BEING TOKED ALL OVER SPAIN FROM BARCELONA TO SEVILLE. ALTHOUGH NOTHING TO WRITE HOME ABOUT, IT DOES THE TRICK WITH A PLEASANTLY MUSKY MELLOW FLAVOUR AND SHORT-LIVED HEADRUSH HIGH. PERFECT FOR THOSE WHO LIKE TO TOKE A LOT BUT NEED TO KEEP A GRIP ON REALITY.

HUEVOS
[MOROCCO]
🌿 🌿 🌿

ANOTHER TYPE OF MOROCCAN HASH SOMETIMES FOUND IN SPAIN IS CALLED HUEVOS. THIS MEANS EGGS IN SPANISH – SO CALLED BECAUSE THIS TYPE TENDS TO COME IN SPHERICAL BALLS THAT ARE POLISHED AND DARK ON THE OUTSIDE, WHILE LIGHTER AND GOOIER WITHIN. LIKE VIRTUALLY ALL THE HASHISH IN SPAIN, HUEVOS COMES FROM THE RIF MOUNTAINS. SMOOTH SMOKE WITH A PLEASANT HEAD HIGH.

MARRAKESH 1
[MOROCCO]
🌿 🌿

STANDARD OFFERING YOU WILL GET IF VISITING THE SOUKS OF MARRAKESH. THESE BLOND SLABS ORIGINATE FROM THE FOOTHILLS OF THE RIF MOUNTAINS WHERE CANNABIS IS THE ONLY VIABLE CASH CROP. THE QUALITY IS BY NO MEANS TOP-NOTCH BUT MARRAKESH 1 HAS A PLEASANT SANDALWOOD FLAVOUR AND AN EXHILARATING EFFECT.

KETAMA
[MOROCCO]
🌿 🌿 🌿

FROM THE KEY HASHISH-PRODUCING AREA HIGH IN THE RIF MOUNTAINS, KETAMA TENDS TO BE DISTINGUISHABLE FROM HASH COMING FROM LOWER ALTITUDES BY ITS DARKER HUE AND MORE PUNGENT, ALMOST MUSK-LIKE, FLAVOUR. IT IS A GOOD DEAL STRONGER THAN THE HASH FROM THE LOWER SLOPES TOO. ITS SMOKE IS PEPPERY AND THICK, ITS SOPORIFIC HIGH ALMOST INSTANTANEOUS.

KETAMA CRUMBLE
[MOROCCO]
🌿 🌿 🌿 🌿

THIS HASH IS NOT SO DENSELY PRESSED AS REGULAR KETAMA HASH AND IN CONSISTENCY IS MIDWAY BETWEEN POLLEN AND HASH. KETAMA CRUMBLE IS ALSO A CUT ABOVE REGULAR KETAMA IN TERMS OF ITS FLAVOUR AND HIGH. ITS SMOKE IS SWEET AND PEACHY AND IT DELIVERS A WONDERFULLY CEREBRAL HIGH THAT IS NOT DEBILITATING. THIS IS A HASH TO TREAT WITH RESPECT.

KING HASSAN
[MOROCCO]

NAMED IN HONOUR OF THE
MOROCCAN KING WHO FINALLY GAVE
THE OFFICIAL GO-AHEAD TO THE
CASH-STRAPPED FARMERS OF THE
RIF MOUNTAINS TO CULTIVATE
MARIJUANA. ITS SMOKE GIVES OFF
A LOVELY FLORAL BOUQUET WHILE
ITS FLAVOUR IS PLUMMY AND
YUMMY. IT DELIVERS A WELL-
BALANCED HIGH BUT, AS WITH SO
MUCH MOROCCAN HASH, THE FIRST
SMOKE IS BY FAR THE BEST.

KING MUHAMMED
[MOROCCO]

ANOTHER REGAL HASH FROM THE
LAND OF THE BERBERS, THIS
PARTICULAR BRAND OF ROCY DOES
NOT QUITE LIVE UP TO ITS PROMISE.
IT HAS A SWEET RICH FLAVOUR AND
A GOOD STRONG HIGH BUT SOMEHOW
FAILS TO ADD UP TO THE SUM OF ITS
PARTS, LEAVING THE TOKERS
DISSATISFIED. SOME CONNOISSEURS
SAY IT IMPROVES WITH AGE.

TANGIER TIGER
[MOROCCO]

IF YOU ARE APPROACHED BY
HASHISH DEALERS ON THE TEEMING
STREETS OF TANGIER, WHICH IN ALL
PROBABILITY YOU WILL BE, THEN
THEY WILL ALMOST CERTAINLY BE
HAWKING TANGIER TIGER – A LOW-
GRADE HASH FARMED IN THE
FOOTHILLS OF THE RIF MOUNTAINS. IT
IS AN UNDISTINGUISHED SMOKE
WHICH TICKLES THE THROAT AND
INDUCES A MILD FUZZY HIGH.

CASABLANCA GOLD
[MOROCCO]

THE CASABLANCANS HAVE GOOD
CONNECTIONS WITH ONE OF THE
BETTER FARMING CONSORTIUMS ON
THE HIGHER SLOPES OF THE RIF
MOUNTAINS. THIS MEANS THAT THE
QUALITY OF CASABLANCA GOLD IS A
CUT ABOVE YOUR AVERAGE. IT HAS A
STRONG FLORAL BOUQUET, DELIVERS
A MELLOW AND FLAVOURSOME
SMOKE AND LEAVES ONE FEELING
THAT GOD'S IN HIS HEAVEN AND
ALL'S RIGHT WITH THE WORLD.

SUPER KETAMA
[MOROCCO]
🌿 🌿 🌿 🌿

TOP-OF-THE-RANGE GEAR FROM THE PEAKS OF THE RIF MOUNTAINS, SUPER KETAMA IS A POLLEN-PACKED HASH WITH A DISTINCTIVE RICH AND SPICY FLAVOUR. IT IS BEST TO RATION THIS STUFF, AS JUST A COUPLE OF HEALTHY TOKES WILL KEEP YOU TOPPED UP FOR HOURS. RARE AS GOLD DUST AND NOT FOR THE FAINT-HEARTED.

ZERO-ZERO
[MOROCCO]
🌿 🌿 🌿 🌿

ANOTHER CLASSIC HASH FROM THE KETAMA REGION, ZERO-ZERO IS THE STUFF OF LEGEND. ONLY THE VERY FINEST POLLEN IS USED IN PREPARING IT AND TRUE ZERO-ZERO WILL CONTAIN ONLY THE BAREST MINIMUM OF LEAF MATERIAL TO BIND THE HASHISH. THIS DELICIOUS BLOND HASH DELIVERS A SILKY SMOOTH SMOKE AND IS GUARANTEED TO BRING YOU TO YOUR KNEES. WORLD CLASS.

MOONSHINE 1
[HOLLAND]
🍁 🍁 🍁 🍁

A NEDERHASH CONFECTION BLENDING POLLEN FROM AK-47, SKUNK 1 AND HAZE. THE RESULT IS AN INCREDIBLY DELICIOUS SMOKE WHOSE MANGO AND CITRUS TONES ARE PERFECTLY COUNTERBALANCED BY ITS VELVETY FULL-ON SPICINESS. THE HIGH VERGES ON THE HALLUCINOGENIC SO MAKE SURE YOU'RE SITTING COMFORTABLY BEFORE YOU FIRE IT UP.

MOONSHINE 2
[HOLLAND]
🍁 🍁 🍁

ANOTHER EXAMPLE OF THE NEW WAVE OF DUTCH HASHISH PIONEERED BY AMSTERDAM'S POLLINATOR COMPANY. THIS COCKTAIL BLENDS ICE, JACK FLASH AND THAI POLLEN, WHICH WHEN PRESSED PRODUCES AN EXOTIC AND TASTY SMOKE WITH A LINGERING AFTERTASTE OF CARDAMOM AND GINGER. YOU FLOAT OFF ON A MELLOW HIGH FOR UP TO THREE MIND-BOGGLING HOURS.

NORTHERN LIGHTS
[HOLLAND]

NORTHERN LIGHTS IS ONE OF THE LEGENDARY SENSIMILLAS, SO IT TAKES A WHILE TO GET YOUR HEAD AROUND THE IDEA OF A NORTHERN LIGHTS HASH – PROBABLY ABOUT THE TIME IT TAKES TO SMOKE A JOINT OF THE STUFF. IN FACT, IT TRANSLATES VERY WELL – ITS MOUTHWATERINGLY RESINOUS FLAVOUR ACQUIRING AN ADDITIONAL POLISH AND DEPTH THROUGH BEING PRESSED. THE HIGH LASTS FOREVER.

WHITE WIDOW
[HOLLAND]

A POPULAR CHOICE FOR MAKING NEDERHASH, BOTH THE PLANT AND THE RESULTING HASH SHARE A FROSTED APPEARANCE. WHITE WIDOW HASH IS A GREAT ALL-ROUNDER. IT MORE THAN LIVES UP TO ITS BEGUILING AROMA, DELIVERING A SMOOTH AND WELL-BALANCED SMOKE WITH SUBTLE FLAVOURS OF SANDALWOOD AND SPINACH. A FEELING OF EUPHORIA CLOAKS THE TOKER.

SHEEBA
[HOLLAND]
🌿 🌿 🌿

SHEEBA SENSIMILLA IS A BEAUTIFUL SMOKE. BUT THE HASH PRODUCED FROM IT DOESN'T QUITE MAKE THE GRADE. IT STILL RETAINS THE MANGO AND CHERRY NOTES. THE HIGH IS STILL UP THERE IN THE STRATOSPHERE, BUT IT'S NOT A PATCH ON THE GRASS. GREAT EXPECTATIONS DASHED. WHAT A BUMMER.

JELLYHASH
[HOLLAND]
🌿 🌿 🌿 🌿 🌿

SIMPLY THE BEST. PRODUCED USING ONLY THE MOST RESINOUS OF THE RESIN GLANDS AND THE REVOLUTIONARY ICE-O-LATOR SYSTEM RECENTLY PIONEERED IN AMSTERDAM, THIS STUFF IS SO STICKY AND POWERFUL IT SHOULD CARRY A GOVERNMENT HEALTH WARNING. IT SPREADS A TAPESTRY OF FLAVOURS ACROSS YOUR TASTEBUDS AND WILL LEAVE YOU AT A LOSS FOR WORDS BUT VERY, VERY HAPPY. LET THE GOOD TIMES ROLL!

93

Chapter 3

Skinning Up

"Victor proceeded to roll the biggest bomber anybody ever saw. He rolled (using brown bag paper) what amounted to a tremendous Corona cigar of tea. It was huge. Dean stared at it, popeyed. Victor lit it and casually passed it around. To drag on this thing was like leaning over a chimney and inhaling."

Jack Kerouac, *On the Road, 1957*

Exploring the many different ways of smoking spliff can be a lot of fun, stretching your ingenuity and imagination to the limit. Joints can be as much an expression of one's personality as a work of art – think Danny the dealer and his Camberwell Carrot in (*Withnail & I*).

This chapter provides a crash course in the origami of joint rolling, from the most basic single-skinner (see below) to the rare and the exotic. This is then rounded off by a whistle-stop tour of the weird and wonderful world of pipes, bongs, chillums and other smoking accessories.

The Single Skin

1. Run a flame up and down a tailor-made cigarette. This toasts the tobacco, making it drier and easier to rub.

2. Tear off a narrow strip of cardboard and roll it into a roach, placing it on the end of a king size paper. Grind the tobacco between thumb and forefinger.

3. Heat the hash (or grind the ganja), then generously sprinkle and rub into the tobacco.

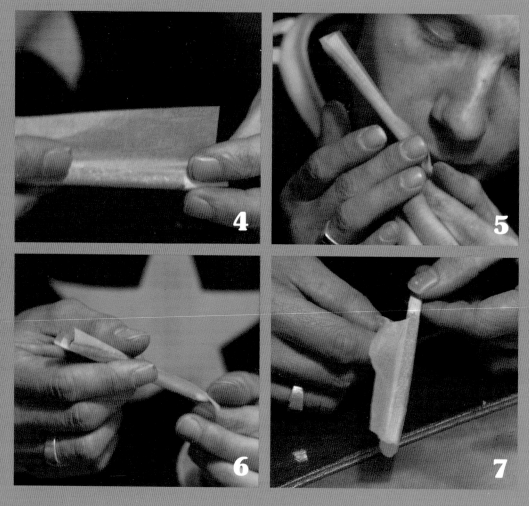

4. Lift up the paper, cradling it between forefingers and thumbs, and gently roll before folding over. This is a knack requiring constant practice.

5. Run the tip of your tongue along the length of the adhesive strip and seal. Don't pack too tightly as this will restrict the passage of air.

6. Run thumb and forefinger gently along the length of the joint to ensure it has stuck, then gently twist the slack paper at the crown to seal the contents in.

7. In cases of mishap or extreme doziness, mount emergency rescue operations with the help of additional papers.

8. When lighting the joint, ensure that you don't pull too hard on it at first. With hash joints, in particular, burning can often be uneven and consequently it is sometimes necessary to apply a little judicious spittle.

9. Enjoy. But don't be a joint hog – remember to pass it round and turn on the neighbours.

Three Skin

The original fatty

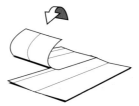

Glue two papers together so you have double the usual width. Gently blow on the glued section until it is dry and secure.

Glue a third paper across the width of the two that are already joined, again gently blowing on the glued papers until they are secure.

Illustrations featured in this chapter are reproduced from *The Joint Rolling Handbook*, published by Bobcat Press.

If you like them short, fat and stubby then the classic three-skinner is the spliff for you. This particular model has a lot to recommend it. In the first place it is idiot proof and extremely straightforward to roll. Doubling up the width of the skins, meanwhile, gives you plenty of room to pack the pot in. That means that there will be lots to go around – easily enough to satisfy two or three seasoned smokers. All these factors make the three-skinner the perfect choice for a coffee morning or to set you up nicely for a night out with friends.

Tear off a strip of cardboard to make a roach filter and mix the marijuana with the tobacco between thumb and forefinger until thoroughly blended.

Position your hands as above, gently rolling the joint between thumb and forefinger to get an even distribution before licking the adhesive strip and folding the paper over.

Screw the excess paper provided by the third paper into a twirl and voilá! All that's left to do now is fire it up and get off your face.

Long Shot

The joint with a point

1

2

Join two skins together lengthwise as above, allowing for a fractional overlap. This is a little fiddly and you need to take care not to lick more of the adhesive strip than you have to.

Add a third skin to the back of the other two papers so that it slightly overlaps them at the bottom. See above.

If you prefer them long and thin to short and fat, skin up a long shot. An obvious advantage of the long shot's length is that when you first light it up you will get a cooler hit because the smoke has further to travel. However, the downside of its skinniness is that the spliff becomes gungier the further down towards the roach you puff. The long shot is sexy and stylish, an elegant-looking smoke that does the job with panache. It's also a doddle to roll. Who could ask for more?

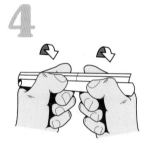

Tear off and roll a short cardboard roach and mix the tobacco and dope thoroughly between forefinger and thumb.

Cradle the joint between your thumbs and gently roll out any unevenness before licking the adhesive strip and folding over.

Fondle gently along adhesive strip to ensure that the joint is sticking securely. Then take a break to admire your handiwork before torching it.

Foxtail Cone

A chillum of a joint

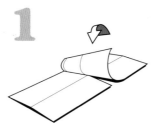

Join two papers together lengthwise by licking the tip of the gum on one of them. Ensure that they are perfectly straight.

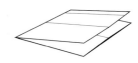

Fold a third paper in half with its adhesive strips facing outwards. Ensure that both sides align.

Keep up the good work by licking and affixing a fifth paper to the top of the broad end of the by now giant paper.

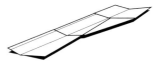

Trim a 45-degree section out of the fourth paper which will aid you in achieving the funnel effect that you are after.

The foxtail cone requires a little more dexterity than the ones we have so far considered but is well worth the effort. Favoured by no less a luminary than Bob Marley, this model works particularly well for grass joints. A grand total of five skins is needed to get it right, so it's not the easiest to roll, but the end result is a magnificently big and bushy spliff.

Lick both sides of adhesive on the third paper before inserting it between the flap of the first two papers as above. Squeeze together.

Withdraw third paper almost instantly and clamp the original two papers together. The glue residue should bind them together.

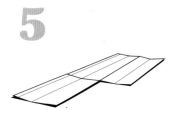

Add a fourth paper to one end of the joined papers by licking adhesive strip and applying to undercarriage, as above.

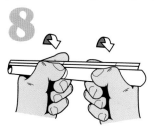

Add contents, mix thoroughly and gently roll out any blockages using the length of both forefingers before folding, licking and sticking.

Twist the twirl end. Your foxtail cone is now ready to embark on active service. Crank up the reggae and fire it up.

Reverse Roll
A joint for flash dudes

1

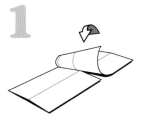

Line up two papers as above. Lick tip of adhesive strip of one and apply to back of other so that there is one long continuous gum strip.

2

Take third paper and fold it in half so that adhesive strips are on the outside. Make sure that the fold is square.

6

Turn the paper upside down with the adhesive strip facing down. Tear off a strip of cardboard to make the roach and then thoroughly mix the ganga or hash in with the tobacco.

7

Roll up as normal but when folding affix the adhesive strip to the underside of the loop after the first rotation, as above.

A word of warning – the reverse roll is one of those party tricks that can go disastrously wrong. If you carry it off with panache you will be feted all round as a hero. But if things go wrong, and they can, you are left with egg on your face and looking like a prize pillock. If you really must show off, at least do a few practice runs at home first.

Lick the adhesive on the two sides of the third paper and sandwich it between the original two as above.

Speedily withdraw third paper before glue dries and use the glue residue to secure the first two papers together.

Run a flame up and down a cigarette, thereby toasting the tobacco inside and making it easier to mix with the dope.

Light the piece of paper left sticking out from the joint before the glue has quite dried. The flame should shoot up the side and self-ignite the joint.

Hey presto you're a hero and everyone wants to take a toke on your reverse-roll wonder joint.

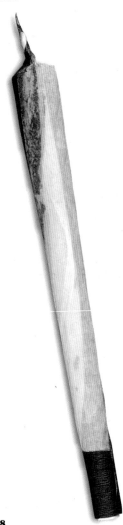

Two-Tone

A sartorial spliff

Join two papers together length-wise. Repeat the exercise with three liquorice papers.

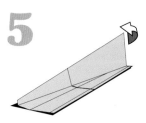

Trim your long liquorice paper by 45 degrees. Retain the section with the adhesive strip.

The two-tone was the joint of choice among the skinheads and early ska fans. Its distinctive two-tone swirl perfectly complemented their fashion foibles and could be seen borne aloft across many a sweaty dancefloor in the late 1960s.

And, although it might require a little time and patience to put together, it more than repays your industry by getting you both mightily stoned and making a stylish fashion statement at the same time.

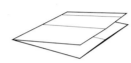

Take a third paper and fold it in half so that adhesive strips are on the outside. Make sure that the fold is square.

Lick the adhesive on the two sides of the third paper and sandwich it between the original two as above. (Repeat for the three liquorice papers)

Speedily withdraw third paper before glue dries and use the glue residue to secure the papers together.

Lick the adhesive strip on the white paper and affix to the liquorice paper as shown above.

Prepare smoking mixture and roll it up as you normally would in your two-tone paper.

Tulip

A flower-power joint

Make a cardboard roach about the length and diameter of a pencil, then wrap, roll and seal with two large papers.

Next take a couple more large papers. Lick the strip of glue on one of them and affix it bumper to bumper with the other one as above.

The slack paper left at the top of the cone can then be gently scrunched up to provide a loose collar as above.

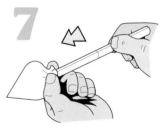

Insert the king-size roach through the collar opening until it is tight up against the dope and tobacco mixture within.

What could be a more perfect vehicle for smoking bud than a tulip? Invented in Amsterdam, hence the name, this joint is easier to build than it might at first look.

And the tulip is not just a novelty spliff either. The extra long roach means it delivers a long, cool, satisfying smoke. Fire one up on a special occasion.

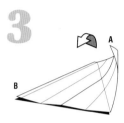

Fold the paper across from A to B as above, while ensuring that the adhesive strip still peeps out above the top of the triangle.

Lick along the adhesive strip, then fold it over and apply pressure to seal. You are now left with a triangle of paper open at one side.

Insert finger and wiggle around to open up the cone and insert well-rubbed dope and tobacco mix. Pack the mix down lightly.

Tighten the paper collar around the roach and secure it with a length of cotton thread so that no smoke can escape.

Light the tip of the cone and puff gently and with caution, teasing the line of the burn with spit until a nice even bonfire is up and running.

Crossroads

The more the merrier

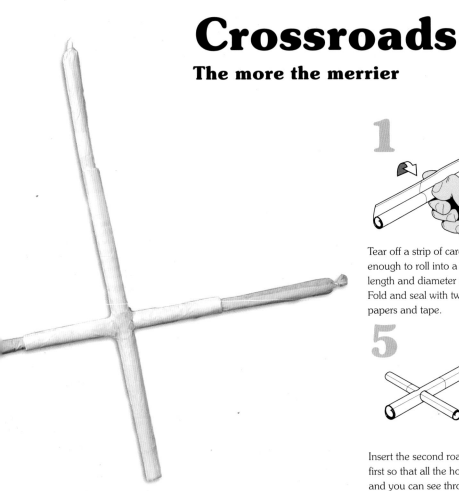

Tear off a strip of cardboard big enough to roll into a roach the length and diameter of a pencil. Fold and seal with two king size papers and tape.

Insert the second roach through the first so that all the holes are lined up and you can see through every chamber.

The crossroads joint is the cannabis equivalent to a cocktail shaker, enabling you to blend a mind-boggling variety of resins and grasses all at the same time. It might be a bit fiddly building this baby in the first place but once you've made the structure it can be used time and again and is sure to afford you hours of harmless entertainment.

Cut a neat circular hole right through both sides of the roach about 3cm from its top. This will eventually form the barrel of the joint.

Make a second roach that is half the length and of a slightly narrower gauge than the original one. Wrap and seal.

Carefully cut the largest possible hole that you can through the centre of the second roach to make a smoke tunnel.

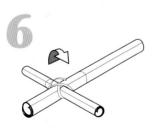

Secure the two roaches with papers and thread. It is important that there is no escape of air as this will impair smoking quality.

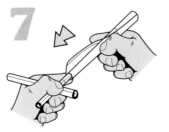

Insert the spliffs of your choice onto the several roach prongs, securing them if necessary with the aid of additional papers.

Unless you have a particularly hearty appetite you would be best advised not to tackle a whole crossroads joint all on your own.

Shiva's Trident

Three times the fun

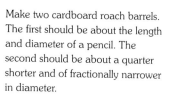

1 Make two cardboard roach barrels. The first should be about the length and diameter of a pencil. The second should be about a quarter shorter and of fractionally narrower in diameter.

2 Take the shorter roach and cut a hole right through its centre and cut two further holes into the top of the roach at each end as shown above.

The dope-smoking sadhus of India carry just three possessions in honour of their master Lord Shiva – their hash stash, a chillum and a trident. This joint is a light-hearted homage to them. It is not easy to build but repays the effort by delivering a smoke of distinction. You can also reuse it. Not one to tackle on your own though – when blasting on all three cylinders the high can become somewhat overwhelming. So invite a couple of friends around to admire your handiwork and help keep the homefire burning. Bom Shiva!

Take the longer roach and cut a hole right through its trunk about 2cm from the top. This should be big enough to snugly allow the shorter roach to fit through.

Insert the shorter roach through the longer roach and position it with all its holes facing up as shown.

Wrap both roaches in papers. Block the holes at each end of the shorter roach with papers or tape, leaving only the three joint holes open. Insert your three spliffs, light up and get high.

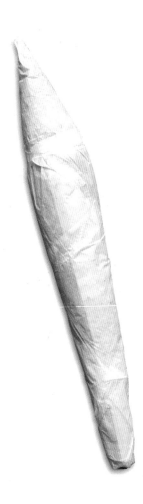

Nosecone

This joint's ballistic!

Stick two king size papers together to make one wide paper, licking the gum strip of one to affix it to the other.

Fold the resulting paper to form a triangle that is just shy of the remaining adhesive strip. Lick the adhesive strip and fold it to seal the flattened cone.

Roll the mixture up into a funnel-shaped joint, which will be topped by a superfluous crown of paper.

Trim both the cone and the joint of superfluous paper. Sandwich the cone to the top of the joint and secure using strips of gum torn from other papers.

You'll be going into orbit with this spliff, which is built along the lines of a military missile. The only difference is that instead of a warhead you've got a weedhead. Chances are that when you take a toke of this you'll decide to make love not war anyway.

Open up the cone and pack gently with a mixture of dope and tobacco. To make it more interesting you can use layers of different blends.

Affix two further king size papers together at roughly a 45-degree angle as above by licking a section of the adhesive strip.

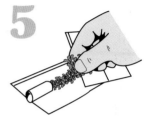

Add a generous cardboard roach filter and prepare an additional and well-rubbed mixture of cannabis and tobacco.

Light the blue touch paper and stand well back. We have lift off!

Lovebud

The soppy spliff

1

Stick two king size papers back to back as above and fold into a triangle, being careful to leave the adhesive strip exposed.

5

Secure your single-skin joints with additional papers.

The lovebud is one for the romantics. But be warned – caution is called for as these contraptions are extremely tricky to get right. Accuracy is of the essence and even a minor mistake can bring the whole structure tumbling down. If in doubt, don't do it and stick with a safer, tried and trusted option. It takes a lot of pot to pack a lovebud and we wouldn't want to see that going to waste. And we don't want to see a beautiful relationship biting the dust either.

Lick the gum and seal into a package.

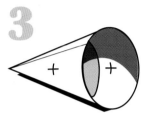

Open up the resulting cone and punch a hole in both sides about halfway down. Make an additional mix of dope and tobacco and again leave to one side.

Make two single skin joints. Snip off the twirly tops off the joints and insert their roaches through the inner holes of the cone until they fit snugly at a 45-degree angle.

Pack smoking mix into the rest of the cone, leaving enough of a paper crown at the top to twirl into a touchpaper.

Light up and pray it doesn't end in tears.

Windmill
Wheel of fire

Tear off a square of cardboard 10cm x 10cm (4in x 4in) and roll it into a cone as above.

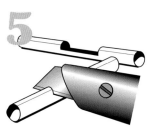

Cut the roach in half and cut the middle section out of each half as above, again using a craft knife.

The windmill is not an easy joint to make and you will need all your skill and ingenuity to get it just right. But it is well worth the effort, providing the ultimate four-way smoke. Get this spliff up and running and your mind will be blowing in the wind for hours to come.

Seal the cone with tape and two king size papers. Leave a 3cm (just over an inch) paper crown at the top of the cone's broadest end.

Make four crosscuts around the cone at regular intervals near the top. You can use a craft knife to make the incisions.

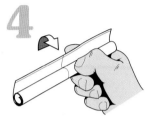

Next make a long, hollow cardboard roach about the length and diameter of a pencil. Wrap in papers and seal with tape.

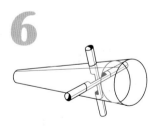

Then carefully insert the two roaches through the crosscuts on the cone so that their roach prongs stick out on either side of the cone as above. Paper and tape to seal.

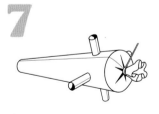

Scrunch the cone's paper crown into a twist and tie securely with thread to ensure no air is getting in.

Insert your choice of four different joints on the roach prongs and secure with papers. Light up and start spinning!

"Marijuana leads to pacifism and communist brainwashing"

Harry Anslinger, Commissioner of Narcotics, 1948

Papers

Skin selection

By far the most popular way of smoking dope is in joints made out of rolling papers. There are innumerable brands of papers on the market and they come in a bewildering variety of shapes and sizes. All the manufacturers strenuously deny that they are targeting the pothead pound with their papers but, particularly in the case of the cannabis-themed and kingsize varieties, such denials smack a little of disingenuousness.

And even granted that some of the more well-known paper brands were originally designed for use with rolling tobacco, purchases by potheads must still account for a sizeable chunk of sales.

Cannabis connoisseurs tend to favour papers made from hemp, while a handy tip if ever caught short in foreign parts is to make your own skins from the rice paper commonly used for packaging rolls of toilet paper. Believe me, man – it really works.

Left: A selection of smoking papers, some made from hemp.
Above: A book of ready-made roaches. Highly recommended to avoid frantic cardboard scrounging.
Right: Pre-rolled cones.

Pipes

Tobacco pipes have been laced with dope from time immemorial, but nowadays pipes are specifically designed with pure dope smoking in mind. These pipes have exceptionally small bowls which are lined with fine mesh filters. These common design elements aside, however, you will be spoiled for choice. Pop down your local head shop and you will be presented with fat pipes, thin pipes, glass pipes, metal pipes, wooden pipes, curly pipes, straight pipes… how are you ever going to decide which is the right model for you? Keep it simple and bear in mind two key factors when making your selection. Firstly, remember that dope pipes frequently clog up with oil. The stem should therefore be of a decent diameter and accessible by pipe cleaner. Secondly, check that the base of the bowl is flat – there is nothing worse than packing a bowl with pot and then having your stash tumble over and spill.

Right and far right: A selection of pipes, ranging from a traditional water pipe to the glass snake that won a Cannabis Cup prize in 2000.

Bongs

From smoke to steam

The bong first impinged on Western cannabis consciousness via American troops returning from Vietnam. The Vietnamese had long smoked bongs fashioned from bamboo.

Like all design classics, the thinking behind the bong is simple. Its central component is a hollow chamber through which the toker inhales. The bowl sits atop a narrow stem jutting out at 45 degrees from near the base of the chamber. The bong is designed as a one-hit pipe for smoking pure ganja or hash. Its main advantages are its economy – none of the dope is wasted – and the purity of flavour it delivers. Since its 1960s debut the bong has been through endless transmogrifications and there are now literally thousands of different models on the market, many of them involving additional chambers filled with water or ice to cool the smoke down.

For a healthier toke, opt for a non-carcinogenic vaporiser bong. Although costing significantly more than conventional bongs, its 'steam smoke' is said to be twice as potent and flavoursome as regular smoke.

Chillums

A social smoke

The chillum is a primitive but highly effective way of smoking a well-rubbed hashish and tobacco mix. Chillums are conical pipes. The best are made from clay and are often embellished with highly ornate carvings. Smoking a chillum is something of a ritual and is only ever done in company. The pipe is held aloft and a small pebble is dropped into its funnel before the dope and tobacco mix is lightly packed in. A wet strip of linen is wrapped around the base stem of the pipe to filter and cool the smoke.

There is a skill to properly smoking a chillum. The stem is first gripped between a thumb and two forefingers. The other hand is then cupped around the first to create a chamber. The toker then rests his head to one side and sucks through his cupped hands as a companion torches the bowl. Such is the volume of smoke generated that head rushes often ensue.

Chillums are widely available at on-line headshops, but if you can't lay your hands on a real one, you can always ad lib one by scooping out a carrot.

DIY smoking

If forced to rely on your own limited resources to get a spliff together, don't despair. There are a number of ways of conjuring up a smoke, almost from thin air, that do not rely on papers or conventional pipes.

The glass lung

The 'glass lung' is one of the simplest tools to create, requiring only a pin, a piece of cardboard and a glass. Insert the pin through the cardboard so that it points up into the air. Impale a small lump of hash on the end and set alight. When burning merrily, blow out the flame and clamp the glass over it until the glass fills with smoke. Cock the glass to inhale the smoke and repeat until it's all gone.

Hot knives

For 'hot knives' you will need a hob, a brace of bone-handled knives, a newspaper funnel and a friend to assist. Your friend heats the knives until they are red hot, then grinds a small lump of hash between them underneath the funnel through which you suck. Snap, crackle and pot. Instant karma.

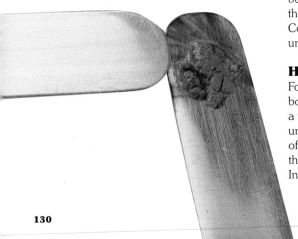

Home-made bongs

There are innumerable ways to make a bong with everyday household items, but the most common method centres around a used soft drinks bottle. You will also need a ballpoint pen, aluminium foil, a needle (or a toothpick) and some used chewing gum or a similar substance.

Use the pen to make a hole in the side of the drinks bottle, approximately a third of the way up from the bottom. Remove the insides of the pen and push its barrel into the bottle, sealing the area around the insertion with the chewing gum. Form a bowl from the aluminum foil and shape it to make a hollow stem at least 2ins (5cm) long. It is essential to make sure that the plastic tube is well protected, as fumes from burning plastic can be extremely noxious. Wrap the foil around the pen. Fill the bottle with cold water so that the bottom of the pen tube is covered. Your bong is now ready for smoking.

Head Shops

Head shops are not, as one might suppose, emporiums devoted to selling shrunken human heads. No, 'head' is here being used to denote drug user, as in pothead. Although other types of heads also use head shops, notably coke heads and acid heads, most of the paying punters are potheads.

Of course, many mainstream tobacconists stock a smattering of kingsize rolling papers and some even offer limited selections of hash pipes and stash tins too. But tobacconists tend to stock other extraneous things too, like chocolate bars and dirty magazines.

The true head shop is an entirely different matter and prides itself on exclusively stocking drug-related products. While it won't actually sell you the pot (although it may well sell seeds so you can grow your own), a well-run head shop will stock every conceivable accessory that a pothead could possibly want: scales, pipes, chillums, bongs, papers, stash boxes, grass grinders… you name it. Typically, the air will be heavy with joss sticks, trance music will be blasting out and you will be invited to browse racks of head fanzines and shelf upon shelf of growing manuals. Other goodies on offer may include brand name seeds and various selections of 'smart drugs' – herbal and chemical combos not currently covered by drug legislation.

Laid-back service

Service in head shops is generally laid back and friendly. Indeed, so pleasant is the buzz that one can't help harbouring a sneaking suspicion that, for all their protestations to the contrary, the people who work in these stores might well be heads themselves.

These people are, of course, in a legally tricky position. Although we know, and they know, that the products they are selling are designed to be used for the consumption of cannabis and other illegal drugs, they will never go on record admitting as much for fear of attracting prosecution. So when taxed about what that Deluxe Space Devil Bubble Bong in the window is for, they get all fidgety and start mumbling incomprehensible things about tobacco. If they stocked hypodermic syringes they'd probably say they were gadgets for icing cakes. Ridiculous – the law is an ass.

Nevertheless, these are the hypocritical lengths that head shops currently have to go to in order to avoid prosecution. This is because, like the coffee shops in Amsterdam, they are occupying a legal limbo. Strictly speaking they are operating outside of the law and their license to trade could be revoked at any moment. They are tolerated, but tolerated only on sufferance. Yet some of them, like Alchemy in London's trendy Portobello Road, are tourist meccas that have been in business for more than 30 years. Alchemy's proprietor, Lee Harris, is a typical head shop owner – a seasoned campaigner for the legalisation of cannabis, whose main claim to fame was being busted for selling rolling papers in 1989. He was sentenced to three months but got off on appeal.

Unfortunately, though, real live head shops like Alchemy are becoming scarcer – their place increasingly taken by new virtual stores on line. These web shops, of course, make good

commercial sense. In the first place, the retailer is far more difficult to track down than one in a conventional store. And they also avoid the embarrassment factor – the furtiveness involved in visiting a real live head shop, like glancing over your shoulder when you slip into a strip show. And, apart from safeguarding the retailer, virtual head shops deliver maximum convenience to the consumer. It's all at your fingertips; a simple click of the mouse will guide you instantly to whatever you want: hemp clothing, drug testing kits, seed suppliers, or the latest in bongs and vaporisers.

Alternatively, of course, you may take pride in your pottiness and be one of those brave souls who still hanker for the human touch and choose to visit head shops in person. If so, just download a directory of stores in your area from the web

Chapter 4

Pot Meets Pop

"Yo man. Open up. It's Dave."

"Dave?"

"Yeah man. It's Dave. Open up."

"Dave's not here."

"What?"

"Dave's not here man."

Cheech & Chong

Pot Meets Pop

Pot made its biggest impact on the Western world during the last century. Although demonised in pulp fiction and B movies during the 1930s and 1940s, its use became fashionable among early black jazz and blues musicians – like Bessie Smith and Louis Armstrong – who found getting high helped them lighten up and get into the swing of marathon jam sessions.

And their passion for pot and jazz was shared by the Beat writers and poets, whose leading lights included Jack Kerouac, Neal Cassady, Ken Kesey and Allan Ginsberg.

And it was the Beats, in turn, who lit the blue touchpaper that was to explode into the anarchic flower power of the 1960s. Suddenly cannabis could be witnessed unfolding in every petal of the blossoming hippie counterculture. Writers wrote about it, singers sang about it and movie makers made movies about it. Pop stars were busted for it and high-brow newspapers began devoting column space to debating its pros and cons. The taboo was broken and cannabis had become mainstream. Later, the coming of the internet in the 1990s only helped matters further by pooling information and rallying supporters together.

The war may not be quite over but any stigma still left lingering around cannabis consumption today is largely restricted to out-of-date and increasingly unenforced pieces of legislation. So indelibly stamped on our culture has cannabis become that it must now rank as the most popular and controversial plant on the planet.

The write stuff

Cannabis first cropped up on the American literary scene in the 1930s and 1940s when featured in a series of sleazy American pulp

Right: Prominent puffer, Louis Armstrong.

fiction works. The most memorable of these was *Reefer Madness* – a lurid melodrama in which a straight A college boy is reduced to wrack and ruin after he becomes addicted to the wicked weed. The book was later made into a low-budget public information film by drug enforcement agencies of the day.

But pot was only to shake off the shackles of pulp fiction and truly make serious literary waves with the coming of a group of writers known as the Beats in the late 1940s.

Jack Kerouac

It was Jack Kerouac who first came up with the 'beat' label in 1948 when he despondently told a friend, 'I guess you might say we're a beat generation.' The Beats developed a style blending stream of consciousness with urgency, often dashing their work out at breakneck speed while chainsmoking joints.

Jack Kerouac, William Burroughs, Allen Ginsberg and Neal Cassady first met at New York's Columbia University in 1948. They soon discovered a shared passion for the black jazz scene of the day, which was centred in New Orleans.

They came from very different backgrounds. Kerouac came from small-town Massachusetts. He was inspired by Cassady's great spirit and the flow of his language – both of which are echoed in the narrative of Kerouac's masterpiece *On The Road*, based on his interstate adventures with Cassady driving the car.

Kerouac wrote the book while high as a kite on pills and dope, scribbling on one continuous ream of paper for nearly a fortnight, pausing neither to correct nor revise. Nobody could make head or tail of it at first and it didn't find a publisher for another seven years. Kerouac remained quite prolific until then but after *On The Road*'s success in 1957 he rather lost the plot, foregoing pot in favour of Thunderbird wine, backing the war in Vietnam and setting himself up as a sworn enemy of the hippies. He finally drank himself to death in 1969 at the age of just 47.

Above: Jack Kerouac, whose *On The Road* became a classic of the beat era.

Williams Burroughs

Burroughs was a different matter entirely. Older and more cynical than the other Beats, he'd enjoyed a privileged St Louis background before attending Harvard. He developed early lifelong interests in crime, guns and drugs. Moving to New York in the mid-1940s he immersed himself in the city's underworld, cultivated a heroin habit and met his common-law wife Joan Vollmer Adams. A few years later they moved to a ramshackle farm in East Texas to farm cotton, oranges and marijuana. Burroughs continued to cultivate his unsavoury habits and Kerouac immortalised the squalor of the place in an episode in *On The Road*. Burroughs then accidentally shot his wife dead while attempting to re-enact the William Tell trick. He fled the scandal, escaping to Tangiers where he was taken under the wing of novelist Paul Bowles. Burroughs developed a flavour for the local majoun cannabis confections and the stubby little kif pipes in which sensimilla is mixed in with strong dark tobacco. It was in Morocco in the mid-1950s that Burroughs wrote his best-known work, *Naked Lunch*. He had just returned to Tangiers from a spell in a London rehab clinic to try to cure him of his heroin addiction. He skinned up dozens of spliffs and racked them up ready for use on the shelf above his desk. Fuelled on a fuggy diet of the joints, majoun and coffee, Burroughs worked maniacally on his manuscript, not even pausing to pick up the sheets of paper as they fell from his typewriter.

"I owe many of the scenes in *Naked Lunch* directly to the use of cannabis"

When later asked of the significance of marijuana in this creative process, he said, 'Unquestionably this drug is very useful to the artist, activating trains of association that would otherwise be inaccessible... I owe many of the scenes in *Naked Lunch* directly to the use of cannabis.'

The work was a heady combo of homoeroticism, violence, cannibalism and drugs.

Drained by his efforts, Burroughs instantly flopped back into his heavy heroin habit. Kerouac and Ginsberg later visited him in Tangiers and helped edit the manuscript. It was Kerouac who came up with the name, remarking, 'The title means exactly what the words say. Naked lunch – a frozen moment when everyone sees what is on the end of every fork.' It was first published in Paris in 1959 but its publication was blocked on grounds of obscenity for several years in the US, though it eventually sold very well there.

Neal Cassady

Neal Cassady wrote very little and is remembered more as the embodiment of the spirit of the Beats than for any literary achievement. Yet he was to become, quite literally, the driving force behind both the Beats and later the hippies.

Cassady was the wild child and muse of the Beats. He originally came from Denver Colorado where he was brought up in a succession of doss houses by an alcoholic father. Early spells in reform school for stealing cars were followed by a series of picaresque hitchhiking trips across the States. Charming and handsome he acquired friends and lovers of both sexes easily and wherever he went.

He first met Kerouac while passing through New York. *On The Road* was based on a series of travelling adventures the two had together with Cassady in the driving seat. Kerouac's alter ego in the book was the narrator Sal Paradise, while he cast Cassady as Dean Moriarty, whom he describes as one of 'the mad ones, the ones who are mad to live, mad to talk, mad to be saved, desirous of everything at the same time, but burn, burn, burn like fabulous yellow candles exploding like spiders across the stars'.

Burroughs, too, employed Cassady's legendary driving skills to transport his marijuana harvests from his Texas farm to New York in the late 1940s. These consignments went smoothly, but Cassady was not always so lucky. One day in the late 1950s he was hitching into San Francisco to go to work. Two guys stopped to give him a ride and it was only when, on parting, he presented them with a joint by way of a thank you that they turned out to be undercover cops. He was busted on the spot and spent two years without the option in San Quentin.

After the success of *On The Road*, Kerouac gave up his cross-country jaunts with Cassady. But Cassady's wanderlust was still very much alive. He became the driver for novelist Ken Kesey and his pot-smoking band of Merry Pranksters who travelled to various drug conventions around the country in an outlandishly daubed psychedelic bus called Further. The early Grateful Dead were often on board to provide the sounds, and sang about the experience in the lines, 'The bus came by and I got on, that's when it all began. There was cowboy Neal at the wheel of the bus to Nevereverland.'

Cassady got busted again for marijuana before ending his days working as a brakeman on the railways on the Californian border with Mexico. His lust for life, travel and cannabis remained undimmed up to his death in 1969. In a fitting

Right: Neal Cassady embodied the spirit of the beat generation.

end, he died as a result of exposure contracted after having fallen unconscious on a 15-mile trek back home after a night of heavy pot partying across the border in Mexico.

Allen Ginsberg

Allen Ginsberg was the poet laureate of the Beat movement. Born in New Jersey to a family of unconventional Russian immigrants in 1927 – his father was a poet and his mother a mentally disturbed nudist – Ginsberg won a place to read law at Columbia but neglected his studies and was soon expelled.

Ginsberg always said that his poetry was born of a vision he experienced one summer's day in 1948 while smoking a joint and reading the works of William Blake. The stuff he was smoking must have been pretty pokey because Ginsberg hallucinated Blake standing before him in the flesh reciting his own lines.

Shortly after this epiphany, Ginsberg was brought back to ground with a bump when he was arrested in connection with one of Burroughs's scams. He found the experience sobering, vowed to mend his ways, started visiting a shrink and got a job advertising toothpaste. It didn't last, though, and by 1955 he'd upped to San Francisco to become part of the burgeoning avant-garde poetry scene there. It was there that he achieved notoriety and

Left: Allen Ginsberg, poet laureate of the 'beat' movement.

success with *Howl*, a raw and angst-ridden poem that opens with the line, 'I saw the best minds of my generation destroyed by madness, starving, hysterical naked.'

However, unlike Kerouac, success did not diminish Ginsberg's relish for the limelight and he went on to successfully make the transition from revered Beat poet of the 1950s to countercultural guru of the 1960s, even coining the expression 'flower power' along the way. He joined Cassady for cross-country jaunts with the Merry Pranksters and tripped out with Timothy Leary. He smoked dope with Bob Dylan and can be seen loitering in an alley in Dylan's seminal 1965 video for 'Subterranean Homesick Blues'.

Ginsberg became a committed cannabis activist. One stunt included pacing the streets of Manhattan with a placard declaring 'Pot is fun'. Another was to go on prime-time TV in 1961 with Norman Mailer saying the same thing. Several years later Ginsberg also published an article called 'The Great Marijuana Hoax'. It was a long rambling piece – he was stoned when he wrote it – railing at the hypocrisy, blindness and stupidity of outlawing pot. He wrote, 'The actual experience of the smoked herb has been completely clouded by a fog of dirty language by the diminishing crowd of fakers who have not had the experience and yet insist on being centres of propaganda about the experience.' Ginsberg particularly deplored classifying the drug as a narcotic and he was to remain fanatically committed to cannabis until his death in 1997.

"No one was safe smoking a joint
in his own home, at any second
20 narcs could bust in guns drawn"

William Burroughs

The Merry Pranksters

Ginsberg's friend Ken Kesey, the madcap leader of the Merry Pranksters, likewise straddled the cusp of the Beats and the hippies. Born in Colorado, Kesey worked as an orderly in a Californian mental hospital in the late 1950s, where he volunteered to act as a guinea pig in some early LSD testings.

The result was his mammothly successful first novel *One Flew Over The Cukoo's Nest*, published in 1962 and later made into a multi-award-winning movie starring Jack Nicholson. Kesey continued writing desultorily but never recaptured his original enthusiasm, preferring instead to channel his energies into masterminding a series of hippie 'happenings' at his Californian ranch involving vast quantities of cannabis and LSD. These came to be known as the West Coast Acid Tests and brought together the nucleus of Kesey's troupe of Pranksters – a loose co-operative of artists, musicians and writers united in little else other than their allegiance to drug taking. Their first outing was a 1964 coast-to-coast drug-fest to visit Kerouac, Ginsberg and Timothy Leary in New York. Cassady, as ever, was at the wheel and Tom Wolfe subsequently chronicled their erratic progress in *The Electric Kool-Aid Acid Test*. Fondly recalling those times, Kesey once said, 'If I could go back in time and trade in certain experiences I've had for the brain cells presumably burned up, it would be a tough decision.'

More cross-country jaunts with the Pranksters followed. Kesey described the rationale behind these trips thus: 'The job is to seek mystery, evoke

"The Pranksters were united in little else other than their allegiance to drug taking..."

mystery, plant a garden in which strange plants grow and mysteries bloom. The need for mystery is greater than the need for an answer.'

It was only a matter of time before Kesey was pulled over in California in 1967 and busted for possession of pot. He jumped bail and fled to Mexico for a while before being recaptured, returning and serving six months. He ended his days buried deep in the country in his beloved Oregon. But right up until his death in 2001 he continued to embark on eventful excursions with his fellow Pranksters. He explained, 'We still stick pretty close together. When you don't know where you're going, you have to stick pretty close together just in case someone gets there.'

Above: The Merry Pranksters prepare their bus –
'Further' – for its drive to the Acid Test Graduation
in San Francisco. With Neal Cassady at the wheel,
this psychedelic monster transported the Pranksters
on frequent drug-fuelled excursions.

Doctor Feelgood

Timothy Leary was a close friend of Ken Kesey and became the self-styled high priest of pot and LSD.

Leary led a colourful life. Born an Irish American Catholic, he later attended the West Point military academy. He became a doctor of psychology after the Second World War at Berkeley California, before moving to Harvard where he began experimenting with mind-bending magic mushrooms from Mexico. The papers got hold of the story and Leary was fired in 1960.

His rehabilitation came thanks to a millionaire philanthropist who set Leary up in his own drug research unit based among the rolling acres of New York's plush Millbrook Estate. It was the perfect spot for Leary to entertain his friends and write *High Priest* and *The Politics Of Ecstasy* – his two psychobabble classics defending the recreational use of cannabis and LSD as mind-expanding substances. It was at Millbrook, too, that Leary coined his famous rallying cry of 'Turn on, tune in, drop out.'

But the busts continued. Millbrook was raided and Leary was pulled over returning from a trip to Mexico in 1965. The police noticed traces of grass in the glove compartment and subsequent body searches revealed a stash of marijuana hidden inside the vagina of Leary's 18-year-old daughter Susan.

Weathermen break out Leary

Despite indignantly protesting in court that he had every moral, professional, political and

"I will miss Tim Leary ... he believed ... as I do that, 'After midnight all things are possible'"

religious right to use cannabis, Leary was convicted and sent down for a ten-year stretch.

But the high jinks didn't end there. With the help of a militant and revolutionary hippie group called the Weathermen, Leary was sprung out of jail. With the aid of a false passport he fled first to Algeria and then on to Afghanistan where he masterminded shipping consignments of hashish back to the United States working with the Brotherhood of Eternal Love – the Californian drug-smuggling cartel.

Busted by the Drug Enforcement Agency in Kabul, Leary was extradited back to America to face trial. Bail was set at $5 million – the largest in US history at the time. He was back in prison again by 1974 but only served three years, snitching up friends and accomplices to the FBI in return for a sentence reduction.

Leary devoted the remaining 12 years of his life to surfing the internet which he hailed as 'the LSD of the future'. When he finally popped his clogs in 1996 his friend the gonzo journalist Hunter S. Thompson wrote, 'I will miss Tim Leary – not for his wisdom or his beauty or his warped lust for combat or because of his wealth or his power or his drugs, but mainly because I won't hear his laughing voice on my midnight telephone anymore ... Tim and I kept the same hours. He believed, as I do, that, "After midnight, all things are possible."'

149

Read all about it

As flower power blossomed and the hippies became more organised a whole new school of journalism emerged catering to the interests of the counterculture.

Oz magazine

One of the most interesting and controversial of these early 'underground' magazines was the full-colour monthly *Oz*, launched by Australian Richard Neville in London in 1967. Although published for just six years, its impact was enormous, its libertarian tone instantly winning it followers among a generation disenchanted with the pedestrian mainstream media of the day.

Oz dared to be different and for the most part got away with it. It was anarchic in tone and style, blending bawdy cartoon strips with scholarly book reviews. It aimed to shock and it succeeded. There was biting satire and caricature, as well as lashings of gratuitous nudity. And it was the first magazine to persistently campaign for the legalisation of cannabis in England.

When its three editors ended up on trial for obscenity at the Old Bailey in 1971 the case became an overnight sensation with 'Free Oz' graffiti scrawled on walls the length and breadth of the land. The court proceedings were farcical, the offending item being a comic strip by American cartoonist Robert Crumb featuring Rupert the Bear indulging in acts of gross indecency with a young lady. The doddery old judge found them all guilty as charged and meted out draconian prison sentences that were quashed on appeal. The magazine limped on for another couple of years, but its spirit had been broken and Neville had lost his appetite for the counterculture, testily voicing his disdain for those who 'burnt you with bad dope, bounced their cheques, jumped your sureties and wrecked your crashpad'. *Oz* folded in 1973 and Neville returned Down Under never to be seen again.

From *Rolling Stone* to *High Times*

Another name to conjure with in the world of underground magazines is the music title *Rolling Stone*. Although it has changed significantly since its 1967 launch in San Francisco and is now more mainstream than underground, it has consistently adopted a pro-marijuana editorial line as well as featuring work positively reeking of the stuff – from the new journalist jottings of Tom Wolfe to the gonzo ramblings of Hunter S. Thompson, who has continued to serve as the magazine's chief political correspondent and roving reporter since its launch.

However, the first magazine specifically devoted to cannabis was *High Times* – a pot fanzine modelled along the lines of *Playboy*. It was the idea of Thomas Forcade, a pot smuggler and entrepreneur, who once remarked, 'Freedom of the press belongs to those who own one.'

Right: (left to right) The *Oz* trio of Richard Neville, Jim Anderson and Felix Dennis.

High Times was launched in 1975 with $20,000 backing. Three years later it was grossing $5 million. Yet despite his business acumen, Forcade was by all accounts a hopeless romantic with a very slender grip on reality. He operated under a number of aliases – his real name was Goodson – and cultivated the air of a dope-dealing devil-may-care international man of mystery for all he was worth. But in reality Forcade was a tortured soul, often prone to bouts of depression. The last straw came when he threw a celebrity party in New York in 1978 and Andy Warhol snubbed him. He never quite got over it and the next week blew his brains out with a pearl-handled pistol. He was only 33.

Twenty-five years on, *High Times* is still going strong and can rightly claim to be the oldest and the boldest of the specialist cannabis magazines on the market.

The king of gonzo

Hunter Stockton Thompson was born in Kentucky and began his career in sports journalism. He once said, 'I rely on my medicine to keep me totally twisted. Otherwise I couldn't stand this bullshit.' By 'medicine' he meant copious quantities of cannabis as well as *every* upper, downer and sidewayser known to man.

Thompson's insatiable appetite for drugs first became apparent in his 1966 book *Hell's Angels*, chronicling a year-long spell on the road with the notorious motorcycle gang. Thompson was clearly impressed by their intake, writing,

'The Angels have no focus at all. They gobble drugs like victims of famine turned loose on rare smorgasbord. They use anything available, and if the result is screaming delirium then so be it.'

Thompson, like the Beats before him, wrote *Hell's Angels* at a frantic pace and on a diet of grass, whisky and speed. It became an instant best-seller and drugs remained a constant theme in all his subsequent writings.

Hunter stands for Freak Power

Apart from drugs and sport, politics was another of Thompson's major preoccupations and in 1970 he formed the Freak Power Party, fielding a string of drugged-up candidates in California, Colorado and Kansas. Thompson himself stood as sheriff in his home town of Aspen Colorado. Describing his electoral strategy, Thompson wrote, 'We ran straight at the bastards from a mescaline platform,' adding sheepishly that 'marijuana got lost in the scramble.' Thompson failed to win office by the smallest of margins, but his political clout had attracted the attention of Jan Wenner – owner of the fledgling *Rolling Stone* magazine – who began commissioning articles from him.

Thompson's most famous book is *Fear And Loathing In Las Vegas*. This is generally regarded as the purest expression of gonzo journalism, or 'impressionistic journalism' as Thompson himself

Right: Hunter S Thompson, the undisputed king of gonzo journalism.

"I'd always done a lot of glue sniffing as a kid. I was very interested in glue. Then I went on to lager and speed and drifted into heroin because as a kid growing up everybody told me, 'Don't smoke marijuana – it will kill you"

Irvine Welsh

described it, in which the author's drug-addled attempts to get a story become more of a story than the story itself.

The book originally grew out of an assignment for *Sports Illustrated* to cover a motorbike race. Thompson wrote about preparing for the journey, 'The trunk of the car looked like a mobile narcotics lab. We had two bags of grass, seventy-five pellets of mescaline, five sheets of high-power blotter acid, a salt shaker half-full of cocaine, and a whole galaxy of multicoloured uppers, downers, screamers, laughers...'

While failing to cover the race, Thompson received an additional commission from *Rolling Stone* to report on a police seminar on Narcotics and Dangerous Drugs. The results were predictably zany. When one of the drug delegates explained that a 'reefer butt is called a "roach"' because it resembles a cockroach,' Thompson protested, 'You'd have to be crazy on acid to think a joint looked like a fucking cockroach.' Which, of course, Thompson was.

Fear and Loathing In Las Vegas was first serialised in *Rolling Stone* magazine before becoming an instant best-seller when published in book form in 1971. Thompson continued reporting on sports, politics and drugs; his gonzo style becoming increasingly erratic and unpredictable. When dispatched to Zaire to cover Muhammad Ali's 'Rumble in the Jungle' with George Foreman in 1974, Thompson didn't even make it to the fight. He later remembered, 'I stayed in my hotel swimming pool... I floated

there naked. I'd thrown a pound and a half of marijuana into the pool – it was together there in a sort of clot, and then it began to spread out in a green slick. It was very luxurious floating in that stuff, though it's not the best way to obtain a high.'

Thompson continues to pump out his highly unconventional brand of journalism at irregular intervals, but only rarely does he now emerge from his heavily fortified mountain hideaway near Aspen Colorado.

Comic capers

Comics are the perfect art form through which to appeal to the very stoned. They don't hang around and can be followed with even the shortest of attention spans.

Pot's pedigree in comic books dates back to 1929 when Popeye was invented by the American cartoonist Elzie Segar. There was definitely something strange about Popeye. He slurred his speech a lot and then there was his inexplicable passion for spinach. Popeye would invariably reach for his stash of the stuff whenever the going got tough – guzzling it down straight from the can or packing a pipe of it in more leisurely moments – and the effect was always miraculous. His spirits would rise and he would suddenly acquire the superhuman strength required to defeat the diabolical Brutus.

However, with the possible exception of *Popeye*, it was the underground comics of the 1960s that were the first to present pot in a positive light.

Mad magazine

The seed of underground comics had been a long time germinating. The first stirring had come with the launch of *Mad* magazine by Harvey Kurtzman in the early 1950s. Quitting *Mad*, Kurtzman had gone on to launch the New York based *Help!* magazine. *Help!* was to have a seminal influence on the world of dope comics.

Robert Crumb, who was working as a schmaltzy greetings card illustrator at the time in Cleveland, Ohio, was so knocked out by *Help!* magazine that he wrote to Kurtzman enclosing some of his early Fritz the Cat doodles about a spliff-smoking feline with an eye'for the ladies. Kurtzman wrote back, 'We really liked the cat cartoons, but we're not sure how we can print them and stay out of jail.' In the event, Kurtzman did run the strip and invited Crumb to join him as his assistant on *Help!*

Crumb's 'Stoned Again'

Robert Crumb was massively inspired by both marijuana and LSD. Many of his most memorable comic characters emerged from a prolonged acid binge he went on in 1966. 'It had this really weird effect,' he remembers. 'It made my brain all fuzzy. It lasted a couple of months and I started getting these images, these cartoon characters.' His cartoon guru Mr Natural dates from this period as does his 'Keep On Truckin'' strip, adopted by The Grateful Dead as their tour logo. However, Crumb's best-known work from this time is undoubtedly his 'Stoned

Harvey Kurtzman, founder of *Mad* magazine.

Again' strip, depicting a hippie's features gradually dissolving into mush across a series of frames as the effects of a spliff kick in. Endlessly reproduced on posters and T-shirts, it became one of the iconic masterpieces of its time – up there with Frank Zappa sitting on a lavatory.

The Fabulous Furry Freak Brothers

Gilbert Shelton was another of Kurtzman's protégés. Shelton was a prodigious toker, once remarking, 'I've always smoked just as much as I could get away with.' And it was in *Help!* that Shelton's cult 'Fabulous Furry Freak Brothers' strip first appeared in 1969. The Freaks were the counterculture's answer to the Three Musketeers. Marijuana was always the catalyst in their adventures as they endlessly pursued elusive dope deals or nubile teenyboppers and were pursued in turn by their square-jawed nemesis Norbert the Narc and his back-up of brutish law enforcement officers.

There was Phineas Freak – sensitive, angst-ridden and forever trying to clean up his act. There was Fat Freddy – a bumbling buffoon constantly getting ripped off on dope deals. Then there was Fat Freddy's incontinent cat who would subsequently enjoy star billing in his own strip. And finally there was the willowy Freewheelin' Franklin whose pronouncement that 'Dope will get you through times of no money better than money will get you through times of no dope' summed up the sentiments of an entire stoned generation.

Above: Fat Freddy's Cat.
Right: The Fabulous Furry Freak Brothers.

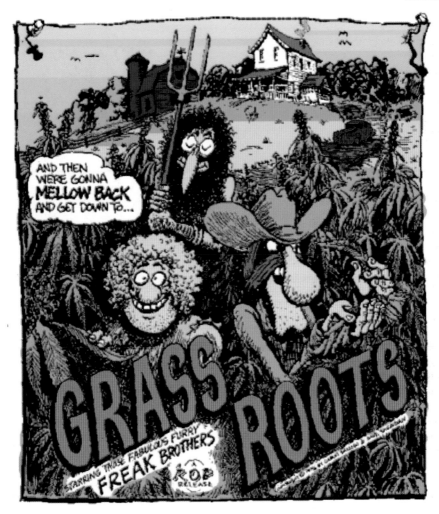

Pacific heights

San Francisco had by now become the hippie mecca of America, with head shops springing up on every street corner. As a result, the city became a magnet for those working in underground dope comics.

Crumb launched *Zap Comix* there in 1967 while Shelton co-founded *Last Gasp* with Ron Turner. Turner remembers the time fondly, 'Back in the late 1960s and early 1970s nearly all the people who read comics were heads. That's how you would turn people on. They would be stoned and you would say, "Hey, read this." People would read a strip by Robert Crumb and they would double over in hysterics, because it would reflect how the mind jumps around when you're high... And that is one of the wonderful things about cartoons, that they can get in there and penetrate with truths when you are stoned.'

Those early underground comic classics by Crumb, Shelton and their ilk remain as fresh and vital today as they ever were. And it is largely thanks to their pioneering efforts that cartoons about pot have since entered the mainstream. Dope smoking regularly featured in Steve Bell's 1980s strip 'Maggie's Farm', whose feline protagonist bore more than a passing resemblance to Crumb's Fritz the Cat. And it's a theme that continues to crop up in Gary Trudeau's world-syndicated 'Doonesbury' strip, in which the perpetually stoned Duke is based on gonzo journalist Hunter S. Thompson.

**Above: Robert Crumb's groundbreaking and influential publication, *Zap Comix* #1.
Right: Much of Crumb's early work was influenced by, or concerned with, drug use.**

Marijuana in the movies

Cannabis made its cinematic debut in the absurdly over-the-top potboiler *Reefer Madness* of 1936. Although the cast was undistinguished and the plot ridiculous, the film remains an interesting period piece reflecting how American public opinion was being prepared for the marijuana prohibition that was to be enacted the following year.

Twelve years later in 1948 the 31-year-old Robert Mitchum was to become a victim of these new laws when busted for dope. Following his arrest, the budding Hollywood star commented, 'I've been using the stuff since I was a kid. It sure beats working.' It was an ill-advised remark and amid the press furore that followed it very nearly cost him his career. Fortunately, though, he found a good lawyer and the case finally fizzled out with an acquittal. Mitchum heaved a heavy sigh of relief and lived to light another joint.

A new cinematic high

However, it was not until the 1960s that dope really made an impact on the big screen. Suddenly it was no longer seen as a menace. Quite the contrary. It was cool and hip – a symbol of the new permissiveness sweeping the nation. It started making cameos in all of the most fashionable films of the day – including Antonioni's *Blow-Up* and Schlesinger's *Midnight Cowboy*. But it was with *Easy Rider* – starring a ridiculously youthful Peter Fonda and Dennis Hopper – that pot really came of age. The plot was virtually non-existent, with Fonda and Hopper doing little more than getting stoned, pondering the meaning of life and gunning their customised Harleys across the American badlands before getting their brains blown out by a couple of bigoted rednecks from the backward Southern states.

Nevertheless *Easy Rider* marked a milestone in cannabis culture. Suddenly dope was big box office and it was OK to feature it in intelligent mainstream films. Alan Parker's *Midnight Express* was a case in point, exploring the plight of a young American tourist caught trying to smuggle dope out of Turkey. His terrifying ordeal at the hands of the Turkish authorities – while in prison he is beaten, tortured and raped – raised important questions regarding the role of the CIA in the American-backed international clampdown on cannabis at the time.

Then there was the whole new genre of war movies made by directors like Francis Ford Coppola and Oliver Stone that exploded onto the scene post Vietnam. Films like *Salvador*, *Apocalypse Now*, *The Deer Hunter* and *Platoon* graphically explored the way in which marijuana was used by soldiers to escape the senseless brutality of war in far-off places. More recently, the actor and prominent cannabis activist Woody Harrelson hit the headlines by outfitting the entire cast of *Welcome To Sarajevo* in hemp clothing.

Right: Robert Mitchum in court in 1948. Over page: (left) *I Love You Alice B Toklas*. (right) *Easy Rider*.

Cheech & Chong

No one rates higher in the pantheon of potheads than Cheech Marin and Tommy Chong, better known as Cheech & Chong.

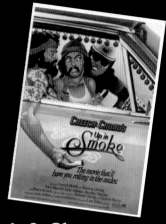

Chong's chilled-out hippie dude was the archetypal airhead and the perfect foil for Cheech's coked-up paranoia. In their 1970s heyday they were the counterculture's answer to Laurel and Hardy.

Cheech's street cred was genuine. He grew up in the crime-ridden hispanic barrios of Los Angeles – an experience later to inspire his Bruce Springsteen tribute *Born in East LA*. It was here too that he picked up his nickname Cheech – a contraction of 'cheecharone', a spicy Mexican snack akin to pork scratchings. He did well at school and sang in a number of nebulous rock bands, including Captain Shagnasty and the Loch Ness Pickles, before moving to Canada in 1968.

Nine-years Cheech's senior, Chong was brought up in Alberta, Canada, the son of a Chinese father and Irish mother. 'He was the first

kind of whatever it is he is that I'd ever seen,' recalls Cheech. Not much of an academic, Chong quit school as soon as he could. 'Most Chinese growing up in Canada held down five jobs and got a degree,' he says. 'Me, I just dropped out and got rich getting stoned.'

After a period flirting with the music business – his high point was co-writing an early Motown hit that was later covered by The Jackson Five – Chong realised that his true vocation lay in stand-up comedy. He put together a troupe of comics and requisitioned his brother's strip club in Vancouver for performances. But he didn't have the heart to fire the girls. 'We had the only topless improvisational theatre in Canada,' he recalls.

Cheech, meanwhile, was working as a local delivery driver and dropped by one night to audition. The chemistry immediately kicked in

nd they were later offered a recording contract.
The rest is hashish history. Their first, eponymous,
lbum of 1971 went gold, their second came
ackaged in a giant rolling paper, while George
Harrison guested as lead guitarist on their third,
which went on to win a Grammy.

Next they turned to the movies, churning out
lmost 20 dope films between 1978 and 1985,
ncluding such cult classics as *Up in Smoke*, *High
Encounters of the Ultimate Kind*, *Still Smokin'*
nd *Far Out Man*. They did cameos too, most
otably in Martin Scorsese's definitive yuppie
ightmare movie of 1985, *After Hours*, in which
hey play a pair of bumbling, blissed-out burglars.
That was their last big-screen appearance together.

There have been the odd one-off TV
ollaborations since, such as when Chong
uested in a 1997 episode of *Nash Bridges* in
which Cheech plays Don Johnson's sidekick.
They were briefly reunited, too, playing
themselves in an episode of *South Park* in 2000.

And Chong has kept the faith, continuing to
tour the stand-up circuit and working on solo
projects such as his *Best Buds* movie of 1998.

But sadly, the magic between Cheech and
Chong has fizzled out. Chong accuses Cheech
of betraying his countercultural roots. The final
nail in the coffin, he says, came when he learnt
Cheech had given up smoking dope. 'Cheech
stopped altogether. He turned, man. We call
those kinds of people "parents". You know
everybody talks about how they don't want to
grow up to be their parents, but some of them,
like Cheech, did.'

The breach seems final. Chong has even started
advertising on the net for a Cheech replacement.

167

Comedy and cannabis

However, it is in the comedy genre that cannabis has enjoyed its finest hour on celluloid. Sean Penn's stoner surf dude in *Fast Times at Ridgemont High* was a tour de force, while Brad Pitt delivered the performance of a lifetime as the bong-blasting couch potato in Tarantino's *True Romance*.

Pot played a starring role too in the whimsical British film *Saving Grace*, which traces the progress of a prim and proper middle-aged

Above: Richard E. Grant reclines with a spliff in a scene from *Withnail & I*.

matron into a very merry widow after she cuts her losses and embarks upon a belated career in dope dealing.

However, the gong for funniest dope film of all time must surely go to *Withnail & I* – an inspired romp through the fag end of the 1960s that follows the fortunes of a pair of out-of-work actors.

The down-at-heel duo score their dope from Danny the dealer – a ludicrously larger-than-life creation whose main claim to fame is the invention of the prodigious 12-skinner Camberwell Carrot joint – 'I invented it in Camberwell and it's shaped like a carrot.' Faultless logic.

Reefer riffs

The connection between marijuana and popular music stretches right back to the turn of the 20th century and the early jazz scene of New Orleans, where potheads were known as 'vipers' and where weed was known under a whole string of aliases including sweet leaf, spinach, muggles, gage, tea, reefer and Mary Jane.

The craze for jazz gradually spread outwards from New Orleans to other urban centres around the US, notably New York, Chicago and Detroit, where it came to be the staple soundtrack played in the mob-controlled speakeasies during the alcohol prohibition years of the 1920s. Louis Armstrong was a regular on the circuit and a great fan of the muggles. In fact, he would later be busted for firing up a joint between sets in the car park of a Hollywood nightclub.

However the main marijuana man of those early jazz years was undoubtedly Milton 'Mezz' Mezzrow (see page 48). Mezzrow came from a white, middle-class Jewish background in Chicago. His first brush with black culture came from a spell spent in reform school after he was busted for joyriding. It was love at first sight.

He later wrote, 'They were my kind of people. And I was going to learn their music and play it for the rest of my days.' Mezzrow duly bought an alto-sax, moved to New York and began picking up gigs in the jazz clubs of Harlem. However, much to his chagrin, Mezzrow never made the grade musically and was to be remembered more for the quality of weed he dealt in than for his music.

Indeed, such was his success in dope dealing that 'Mezz' passed into the jazz vernacular as a synonym for top quality gear. His grass even came to be celebrated in song in the classic 1938 composition 'If You're A Viper', which featured the following lines:

'Dreamed about a reefer five foot long
The mighty mezz, but not too strong...
I'm the king of everything...
If you're a viper.'

Rock and rollers

Although remaining a staple diet of the jazz world, Elvis famously 'despised' pot and it rather fell out of favour in the rock and roll years of the 1950s.

But all this was to change with the coming of flower power and the Swinging sixties. Pot exerted an influence on virtually every area of popular culture during those years, but especially so in music.

Bob Dylan was probably first turned on by his friend the Beat poet Allen Ginsberg. Dylan became a firm convert and one of the weed's most vocal champions, insisting in song that, 'Everybody must get stoned.'

"What is a weed?
A plant whose virtues have
not yet been discovered."

Ralph Waldo Emerson

Dylan inspires Fab Four

It was Dylan too who turned on The Beatles. The story goes that the Fab Four had been playing a concert in upstate New York in 1964. Lennon was a great Dylan fan and after the gig asked a reporter to arrange an audience with his hero. A call was made and Dylan subsequently rolled up a little the worse for wear and bearing a big bag of grass. The meeting was a real eye-opener for the naïve Liverpudlians, whose experiences with drugs up until then had been limited to purple heart speed pills. McCartney later recalled, 'We were kind of proud to have been introduced to pot by Dylan, that was rather a coup. It was like being introduced to meditation and given your mantra by Maharishi. There was a certain status to it.'

Back in England the following year, John, Paul, George and Ringo were summoned to Buckingham Palace to be awarded MBEs. Rumour had it that they slipped off into an antechamber to share a spliff before being ushered into the presence of Her Royal Highness.

Two years later, in 1967, *Sergeant Pepper's Lonely Hearts Club Band* was topping the charts – The Beatles' most overtly druggy album to date, featuring lyrics such as, 'Picture yourself in a boat on a river/With tangerine dreams and marmalade skies.' That same year, in July, they all became signatories of the famous full-page ad in *The Times* headed, 'The law against marijuana is immoral in principal and unworkable in practice.'

Brushes with the law were to follow. John was busted for hash the following year in a raid involving 40 officers – raising questions in parliament as to why so many were needed to detain one unarmed suspect. George was raided in a later incident, while Paul was busted no less than five times over the next few years.

Roll away the Stones

However, by far the most famous cannabis bust of the 1960s, and the one that attracted the most prurient publicity, involved The Rolling Stones. This took place in February 1967 when police swooped on Redlands – Keith Richards' country house in West Sussex. There was a party in progress. George Harrison had just left but guests still remaining included the art dealer Robert Fraser, as well Mick Jagger with his then girlfriend Marianne Faithfull. Cannabis and amphetamines were seized. Richards, Jagger and Fraser all ended up being charged in what was to become a cause célèbre. The tabloids had a field day, their interest becoming positively frenzied when rumours began circulating that Jagger had been surprised in flagrante performing a sweet-toothed act of cunnilingus on Faithfull involving a chocolate bar. The broadsheets proved less salacious and more sympathetic with *The Times*, depicting Jagger as a scapegoat in its famous 'Who Breaks A Butterfly On A Wheel?' editorial. In the event, Richards' 12-months was quashed on appeal, while Jagger escaped with a conditional discharge.

Right: Bob Dylan turned The Beatles on to pot.

Trenchtown rock

While it was American and British rock idols who put pot on the map in the 1960s, the tide of cannabis culture was to change in the 1970s.

Ganja had long featured prominently in Jamaican culture. The quasi-religious rastafarian movement regarded 'the holy herb' as a sacrament and it was smoked fanatically by the resident rastas of Kingston's ramshackle Trenchtown district.

However, it was not until Bob Marley and the Wailers released their *Catch A Fire* debut album in 1973 that the world started taking notice of what was going on there. Marley smoked ganja with a religious zeal and was truly a man with a marijuana mission. He would fire up at the slightest pretext, often on stage, and several of his songs specifically paid homage to dope, notably 'African Herbsman' and 'Kaya'.

Marley once said, 'When you smoke herb, herb reveal itself to you. All the wickedness you do, the herb reveal itself to yourself, your conscience, show up yourself clear, because herb make you meditate. Is only a natural t'ing and it grow like a tree.'

Between his taking up the habit in 1966 and his untimely death in 1980 experts estimate that Marley smoked his way through a staggering stash of 300kg of prime Jamaican bud. In was entirely appropriate and in keeping with the man that, at his state funeral in 1980, Marley was finally laid to rest with a big smile on his face and clutching a bouquet of his beloved ganja.

"Marley smoked his way through 300kg of prime Jamaican bud"

Peter Tosh

No less evangelical in his commitment to cannabis was fellow Jamaican reggae artist Peter Tosh – one of the early Wailers who split with the band to pursue his own solo career. Tosh, like Marley, was a tireless campaigner for worldwide legalisation of cannabis. However, his style was more militant and confrontational than that of Marley, and following the release of his uncompromising *Legalise It* album of 1976 he became the bloodied but unbowed victim of a systematic campaign of police brutality and beatings. In an interview he gave in 1987, Tosh said, 'If gunmen come tomorrow to get I, I'm not afraid. Jah will protect I.' Those words were to prove eerily prophetic when later that year Tosh was gunned down in his own home at the age of 43. A true marijuana martyr.

Right: Peter Tosh partakes of the herb.

Mr Nice

Howard Marks was born into a modest Welsh background and won a place to study physics at Oxford University in the early 1960s. It was at Oxford that Marks embarked on his long and distinguished career as one of the most celebrated dope dealers of all time.

From Oxford, Marks moved to London, where the quantities of dope involved got progressively larger. The next step was smuggling, an activity in which Marks proved himself extremely adept. He quickly built up a powerful international network of friends and contacts in organisations as varied as the IRA, the CIA and MI6. One typically audacious operation involved Marks identifying a glut of Colombian grass being smuggled into Miami by the Mafia. Prices were plummeting. So Marks started shipping over hashish and Thai sticks instead. He charged five times the going rate for Colombian and made a killing.

But his luck finally ran out in 1979 when he was busted in England for running dope and using a false passport. He served three years before returning to smuggling with a vengeance. By the mid-1980s Marks had 89 phone lines, 25 companies and 48 aliases, among them Mr Nice. He owned bars, nightclubs, brothels and travel agencies all over the world, which provided useful fronts for money laundering his ill-gotten gains and disguising his core dope-dealing business.

At his peak, Marks was smuggling 30-ton consignments of cannabis from Pakistan and Thailand to America and Canada by land, sea and air on a regular basis.

But this had not escaped the notice of the agents of the American Drug Enforcement Agency, who finally nabbed their man in the late 1980s. Marks was sentenced to 25 years at the Terre Haute Penitentiary in Indiana. He served seven of them before his release in 1995, when he returned to the UK to write a best-selling autobiography, stand as a pro-cannabis MP and set up the Mr Nice Seed Bank.

Chapter 5

Dutch
Blooms

"I hate to advocate drugs, alcohol, violence or insanity to anyone, but they've always worked for me"

Hunter S. Thompson

Dutch Blooms

Fresh air fanatics are few and far between in the Netherlands, where no-smoking restrictions would prove as unworkable as a ban on clogs or tulips.

You have got to hand it to them, the Dutch are champion tobacco smokers. Great billows of smoke assail you from all sides in Holland, the partakers sucking equally contentedly on cigarettes, pipes or cigars. However, their especial favourites are roll-ups packed with pungent Dutch shag tobacco. Indeed, such is their passion for puffing, it comes as no surprise to learn that the expression 'Dutch fuck' is a euphemism for chainsmoking by lighting each successive cigarette from the smouldering stub of its predecessor.

And this enthusiasm for smoking tobacco has been extended to cannabis, which the Dutch likewise consume prodigiously and in as equally inventive different ways. Cannabis has long played a key role in Dutch culture and commerce. Nowhere is this more evident than in Amsterdam – the cannabis capital of the world – where huge clouds of aromatic spliff smoke often sweep across your path. A whiff of weed here, a hint of hash there.

Cannabis and its ready availability has become something of a symbol of the place – along with the trams trundling by and the prostitutes seated provocatively in windows. Indeed, such is the importance of cannabis to the Dutch economy that a government survey in the 1990s ranked it as one of the country's top five cash crops, along with tomatoes and cut flowers.

Above: Amsterdam's Cannabis College.

Droves of tourists flock to Amsterdam from all over the world to get mightily wrecked. They skin up spliffs and nibble space cakes in the coffee shops, marvelling over the menus offering many different exotic strains. They stock up on top-quality seeds at one or other of the dozen or so reputable chandlers who, like the coffee shops, openly do business around the city. They browse the headshops – one on every high street – where they trawl the latest in bongs and vaporiser pipes before stocking up on sachets of mind-bending magic mushrooms.

They make the obligatory pilgrimage to the cannabis conurbation on the edge of the red-light district, where they check out the latest goodies on offer at the Sensi Seed Bank, brush up on their history at the Hash Marijuana Hemp Museum or attend seminars at the neighbouring Cannabis College. They buy the T-shirts, the vaporisers and the fancy glass pipes.

They sip cannabis-based cocktails, beers or wines at the bar of the Hemp Hotel and dine out at one of the many restaurants to feature dope-laced 'specials' on their menus.

Finally they get blitzed at one of the many coffee shops scattered around town before making their unsteady way to the legendary Milkyway nightclub to toke in the new day.

181

Café Society

There are nearly 300 coffee shops in Amsterdam, identifiable by a distinctive green logo in their window and range, from cosy and intimate to big and brash.

Although their early history is hazy, the Bulldog Coffee Shop in the city's ancient red light district that opened in 1975, is generally acknowledged as being the first outlet to actually describe itself as a coffee shop and openly sell hashish on the premises.

The brainchild of Dutch entrepreneur Henk de Vries, the Bulldog has since gone on to become the biggest of the chains and an extremely lucrative business. The Bulldog might have formularised the idea of the coffee shop, but little bars or tearooms where smoking and dealing were tolerated had already started appearing in the late 1960s.

Most coffee shops today will offer at least half a dozen different varieties of grass or hash, mostly sold from dealer booths in pre-packed plastic bags of two or three grams (1/8oz). There is no haggling involved, as on the black market, and the prices of the different types, along with tasting notes, are clearly marked on laminated menus.

Loose joints, space cakes and shakes, magic mushroom teas, branded drug paraphernalia and souvenirs are also often on sale. Rolling papers and roach material are generally laid on free of charge, as is use of house bongs and vaporiser pipes.

Most of the staff and clientele are young, the decoration often themed, and loud music is just one of the factors making conversation difficult. Lighting is low and visibility is further impaired by the regular eruption of smoky volcanoes amidst the glassy-eyed visitors sprawled, as often as not, among giant fluorescent floor cushions. Bloodshot eyes smart in the impenetrable haze and nostrils quiver at a seemingly endless aural collage of heady scents and exotic aromas. The coffee shop is a stroppy teenager's dream bedroom come true.

Although, according to the letter of the law, the sale of cannabis is illegal in the Netherlands, coffee shops plying a trade in the drug are

nevertheless tolerated and even licensed by the Dutch authorities.

Legal limbo

Officially, though, they don't exist, consigned to a Kafkaesque twilight zone where nothing quite adds up. This atmosphere of legal limbo breeds myths and distortions, while also feeding the latent paranoia of the coffee shop staff. Owners often grumble that they are hard done by; that, in spite of being licensed and wanting to be wholly above board, they are being victimised and forced to operate clandestinely. They cite the severe penalties their suppliers face if caught, and the recent outlawing of all indoor cultivation as conspiring to put them out of business. They complain, too, that the authorities are increasingly revoking alcohol licenses – representing a severe drain in revenue. And they say the 5g (less than 1/4oz) limit for personal possession of cannabis and the 500g (just over 1lb) limit for retailers are

both ridiculous and unworkable. They mutter darkly about troubled times ahead.

Yet, on closer inspection, all this bellyaching is really so much hot air. Business appears to be booming and the choice of top-quality spliff is wider than ever before.

Indoor grow plots are commonplace around the city – indeed, some are on public display. And anyone can see that the 5g and 500g limits are routinely flouted with complete impunity, as is the 'no advertising' rule.

Yet there are changes afoot. Imported hashish is becoming increasingly scarce as home-produced pot becomes increasingly commonplace. And there does appear to be some hardening of official attitudes towards the trade. However, whatever the legislators ultimately choose to do and whichever way the space cookie crumbles, one thing is for sure – the coffee shop is too ingrained into the everyday life of Amsterdam ever to be completely eradicated.

Cream of the Coffee Shops

Amsterdam's coffee shops are places where you can buy and consume cannabis free from paranoia, in the company of civilised, like-minded folk.

There are nearly 300 coffee shops in the city, ranging from trashy tourist traps aimed at the marijuana equivalent of lager louts to super-trendy establishments for Amsterdam's ultra-chic. The following are a selection of some of the best, where you will find a wide selection of grass and hash. Many of them also offer pre-rolled joints and space cakes. Prices vary according to the strength, strain and rarity value. It's generally considered polite to eat or drink something while visiting coffee shops, but protocol can vary. Some shops have licenses to sell alcohol but these are increasingly being revoked when they come up for renewal.

Barney's Breakfast Bar
Haarlemmerstraat 102

Barney's lives up to its name: this is the best place to go for a hearty, English-style breakfast (eggs, bacon, sausages – the works), making mornings the busiest time to visit. Food-wise, there are vegetarian and vegan options.
As for the *other* menu, the selection is equally impressive (excellent Northern Lights, similarly good White Widow). This is one of the few places where you can combine an English breakfast tea with superlative Morning Glory – a 2002 Cannabis Cup winner. Barney's also scooped the best coffee shop gong in 2002 to add to the many others it had won in previous years. Barney's proprietor is actually Derry, an Irishman who has run the place for years. The shop was refurbished at the end of 1999, and is now a light, airy venue. Derry has forged strong alliances with a handful of small growers who now sell exclusively through him.

Blue Bird
Sint Antoniesbreestraat 71

This coffee shop has garnered a worldwide following, thanks to its wide range of grass and hash and multi-lingual staff. It occupies a modern building in the old Jodenhoek (Jewish district) with a glass-plated frontage. Inside the layout is split-level, with hand-painted murals. The ground floor houses the coffee bar, while upstairs is a

Above: Dealing counters in coffee shops vary from highly organised operations like this one to rather more rudimentary affairs.

further café and dealer's counter. Next to the latter is a chill-out area with a big squashy couch for sitting back and getting zonked on. The Blue Bird is famous for its menus, which take the form of two huge books – *Plants of the Gods* for grass and *Book of Dreams* for hash. The nearby University of Amsterdam accounts for the large number of students who frequent the place.

Brandend Zand
Marnixtraat 92

This coffee shop has won plaudits for its architect-designed interior, which includes a huge fish tank, dark blue glass steps, three different seating areas (one of which features giant couches on which to sprawl) and a poolroom with overhead skylight. The thought that went into the design and layout of the place is equally evident in the menu, which is made up of ten consistently reliable varieties of grass, and 11 of hash. Bio Haze is a house speciality.

The Bulldog
Oudezijds Voorburgwal 90

Although something of a tourist trap, this place
is worth visiting for its historical associations
alone. When the original red-light district branch
opened back in 1975 it was the first place in
Amsterdam to call itself a coffee shop and openly
trade in dope. Nowadays, The Bulldog is a
veritable empire, complete with its own range
of branded merchandise. And the original branch
has become something of an Amsterdam cliché
(sex and drugs rubbing shoulders).

Apart from the red-light district branch, The
Bulldog chain now encompasses The Bulldog
Lounge (formerly 7th Heaven) at Spuistraat 7
and the Bulldog Palace at Leidseplein 17 which
is housed in a former police station.

De Dampkring
Handboogstraat 29

You can't walk past this centrally located
establishment in the Spui area (above): the
colourful façade with its moulded, studded iron
grilles is guaranteed to pull you in. And once
inside, the visitor is welcomed by one of the best
menus on offer in Amsterdam, with no fewer
than 23 varieties of grass, 18 of hash and ten
choices of pre-rolled joints (including two pure
varieties). Each is classified according to type,
origin, taste and high. The 'fair smoke'
denomination is awarded to pot produced by
small homegrowers. Alcohol is available here,
as are good munchies, juices and shakes.

The Dolphin
Kerkstraat 39

Popular with Americans and a strong Cannabis Cup contender (it came second in the hashish category in 2000 and third in the coffee shop category in 2002) this small coffee shop has an authentic Dutch feel to it. It is only a short walk from the Leidseplein, and devotees rate its winning combination of good music, good buds and good hash, although the menu is limited to four varieties of each.

The aquatic theme is reflected in the décor. And the Dolphin is branching out these days, having teamed up with a canal boat company to offer smokers' cruises.

Dread Rock
Oudezijds Voorburgwal 67

As the name suggests, this coffee shop offers reggae aplenty (although not exclusively; hip-hop, Latin sounds and club DJs also feature). It's a classy venue in the middle of the red-light district – an area not renowned for its rich coffee shop pickings. Mirtel, the owner, has a policy to buy cheap but carefully, and she does both with aplomb. White Widow, Shiva, and Super Skunk are her most popular smokes. The White Widow weed won third place in the Cannabis Cup in 1998. You can also find good Nederhash here. There are also two full-sized pool tables.

Dutch Flowers
Singel 387

This well-known coffee shop benefits from a prime location on Singel with fine views, and it specialises in quality hash and weed. Its Unique took first place in the Cannabis Cup hashish category in 1999, while its Dutch Night Nederhash came third in 1997 and second in 1996.

Free I
Reguliersdwarsstraat 70

Named after Free I Dixon – who, along with Peter Tosh, was shot in 1987 – Free I is one of the oldest registered coffee shops in Amsterdam. The Jamaican nuances are carried over in the tropical-style décor, with bamboo and lush fronds of greenery dominating the small interior. The menu comprises ten weed and ten hash varieties, many of them organic. The powerful Spice Ice hash is not for the fainthearted. On the weed side, smokers can choose between White Widow, White Russian or Power Haze. A curious happy hour operates every day between 12pm and 2pm and from 6pm till 8pm when every 2g purchase of grass is supplemented with an extra 1g free.

Greenhouse
Tolstraat 91

This is the original Greenhouse, now one of a chain of three. Although the flagship of the empire, Greenhouse Tolstraat is well off the beaten track, south of Sarphatipark. This is a smart, top-notch coffee shop with the atmosphere of a swanky private club, complete with leather-upholstered chairs, couches and table service. You get your hash and grass from a bar just inside the main door. Entrance into the lounge area requires a membership pass for locals, although tourists can come and go freely. The list of Cannabis Cup awards this coffee shop has won is never-ending, with more than half of the hash and grass offerings (including ten bio varieties of grass) having scooped medals.

Grey Area
Oude Leliestraat 2

This minuscule place has achieved cult status, having for years been the 'underground' smoking haven of those in the know, and famous as the home turf of AK-47 (which more than lives up to its killer name), Bubblegum, Yellow Cab and Grey Mist. The ceiling air filters are welcome in light of the place's tiny size (15 is a squeeze). Deals in US-style eighths (3.5g) are available, as are 4.20g specials (named after the time of the clock on the wall, which is frozen) from the two perpetually stoned and enthusiastic proprietors. Although principally a weed venue, they do get some tasty Moroccan hash from time to time.

Homegrown Fantasy Lounge
Nieuwezijds Voorburgwal 87a

An aptly named coffee shop that prides itself on buying direct from small homegrowers and avoiding smuggled gear. Grass is the house speciality and it tends to be extremely potent. All the grasses are organically grown and there are 15 indoor and four outdoor varieties available from behind the bar. Most famous is the legendary Jack Herer, plus the Haze/Skunk hybrid which won the top Cannabis Cup prize in 1992. The shop's space cakes are said to be the strongest in Amsterdam. The place is also an art gallery, and something of a showcase for the company's sister outfit, Homegrown Fantaseeds. It's a little hard to find the coffee shop – keep your eyes peeled for the old-style sign that hangs outside.

Kashmir Lounge
Jan Pieter Heijestraat 85/87

For laid-back seating arrangements, the Kashmir has got things properly sussed. Its main room is

A bit of Eastern delight at the Kashmir Lounge.

scattered with a sea of cushions and pillows from which poke out little islands of low tables. Further back there are two more seating areas, where there are couches and ornate chairs. The nicely balanced menu has ten weed (including bio Skunk) and ten hash varieties. The Nederhash Dutch Delight is a particularly popular option. The reputation of this place just seems to grow and grow with its relaxed atmosphere attracting a tremendous mix of punters. But it still somehow manages to retain a local feel.

De Kuil
Oudebrugsteeg 27
This venerable establishment has been a bar for more than 100 years and has had the same name – which means cowl – throughout that time. It has also retained its traditional Amsterdam atmosphere, with an antique bar and oak beams running all the way round to the pool table area

at the back. The shop appeals to a slightly older clientele than usual who can often be found enjoying civilised spliffs and cold beers. The music is mainly 1960s and 1970s, with regular doses of Zappa. The menu isn't particularly large or prize-winning, but the pot is always reliable and the place has a welcome bring-your-own-food policy.

Het Kruydenhuys
Keizersgracht 665

This coffee shop on the picturesque Keizersgracht has won several Cannabis Cups for best coffee shop. Formerly known as Lucky Mothers, Het Kruydenhuys has a reputation for good food, good views (chairs and tables look down on a canal) and good weed (Mother's Milk and Bubblegum are both former Cannabis Cup winners). The place feels as though it has been preserved in aspic since the 1960s and maintains its 'love and peace' ethos on one of the most beautiful canals in Amsterdam.

The Noon
Zieseniskade 22

This small shop is located in a quiet backwater between the Rijksmuseum and Leidseplein. What it lacks in size, however, it makes up for in quality, offering plenty of bio weed and a good supply of glass bongs (which you can use to try out potential purchases *gratis* before you buy). The American proprietor ensures that the weed is properly cured. Both Edelweiss and Dusty are on the menu, as is former Cannabis Cup winner Blueberry.

Old Church
Oude Kerksplein 54

Situated in one of Amsterdam's most famous old squares in the heart of the red-light district (opposite the real Old Church), this place is a honey pot for tourists. The menu stretches to seven varieties of weed, including one bio variety, and six of hash. Established in 1983, this is one of the city's earlier coffee shops. The décor is traditional, with sober colours, smoked glass and dark wood throughout. There is an upstairs seating area that provides a good perch from which to watch the world go by.

De Rockerij

This is the original Rockerij (the others are Rockerij II and III), a stone's throw from Leidseplein. This dark, cave-like place has become a byword for quality weed and hashish.

Coffee with green ... a classic combination.

It has a seemingly inexhaustible supply of top-class Moroccan hash (in 1998 it came third in the Cannabis Cup hashish category with its Rockerij Special import), and several strains of its weed (Bubblegum, AK-47, White Russian) have also won gongs. Prices are fair, thanks to a conscious move by the owners to reduce mark-ups. The décor was overhauled in 1996, and the result is a panoply of Asian and Indian influences. Passing tattoo artists and tarot-card readers only add to the bazaar-like Eastern atmosphere.

The Rookies
Korte Leidsedwarsstraat 145-147

Close to the Leidseplein, this roomy shop has lots of tables and chairs and can comfortably accommodate up to 80 people. At one time, its proprietors were the youngest coffee shop owners in the city – hence the name. Since which time, however, they have turned out to be consummate pros. The place has lots of wood (the bar runs the whole length of the shop) and, with posters and arty designs decking the walls, the feel is that of an authentic café-bar. The menu has seven varieties of grass (all biologically grown) and five of hash. Bongs are available, as are pre-rolled joints (with or without tobacco), plus there is a pool table and fully-stocked bar.

Rusland
Rusland 16

Acknowledged as one of the oldest coffee shops in Amsterdam, Rusland is nonetheless a far cry from the old Dutch-style café-bars. The theme throughout is unmistakably Russian, both in colour (red, gold and purple dominate) and choice of artwork (pictures of Orthodox churches hang on the walls). A focal point is the huge display cabinet filled with glass pipes. Though a well-established shop, Rusland was a latecomer to the Cannabis Cup competition – first entering in 2002. The dealers, however, are extremely knowledgeable about their smokes; the menu has ten varieties of grass and nine of hash. Different seating areas are spread over three levels (the upstairs bar is where you select your cannabis). A wide selection of teas (42 different types) is also available, as are cannabis seeds from five different companies.

Siberië
Brouwersgracht 11

With its diverse clientele (business folk, media types, students) art exhibitions and laid-back atmosphere, this relaxed neighbourhood shop on the picturesque Brouwersgracht could have been transported straight from the 1960s but was in fact founded in 1984. Siberië offers a wide selection of cannabis, with two Cannabis Cup-winning strains (Siberian Tiger hydro-weed in 1998 and Amsterdam Delight Nederhash in 1996). The owners, formerly of Rusland, have opened two further coffee shops in the same mould: the Republiek and De Supermarkt.

Softland
Spuistraat 222

At Softland you can surf the net while getting stoned at the same time. It's a bright, ultra-modern coffee shop in the Spui district set up by a founder member of the Interpolm grow shop, who now supervises the growing side of the business. The name was chosen to reflect the fact that the shop sells both soft drugs and soft drinks. The weeds here include bio and hydro varieties, but the main attraction is the space cakes and shakes, the latter coming in a variety of flavours.

Tweede Kamer
Heisteeg 6

This coffee shop is the sister business of De Dampkring. It is one of Amsterdam's most reliable venues for hashish and has been a favourite among locals in the know since it opened in 1985. With dark panelling throughout, the Tweede Kamer (the name means 'second room') has all the cosiness of a traditional Dutch cafe. The staff are exceptionally knowledgeable and full of enthusiasm. The menu is varied and includes some of the best sensi in town, including NYC Diesel.

"They've outlawed the number one vegetable on the planet."

Timothy Leary

Hashish haven

The Pollinator Company is housed in a quiet canalside warehouse just a couple of blocks away from the crowds and trams of Amsterdam's bustling Rembrandtsplein. There is no intercom and the rickety front door is unlocked. A prefab reception area opens into a room the size of a car park. Crossing the threshold, the stench of cannabis hits you like a cosh. Clouds of deep blue smoke waft and mingle – a spicy whiff of Afghani black hash here; a sweet swirl of Northern Lights grass there.

Marijuana posters plaster the walls along with glass cases containing a bewildering variety of smoking paraphernalia, specimen cases, board games and other cannabis-themed merchandise. In no discernible order, brightly coloured displays of pipes and bongs adjoin stacks of cannabis-related books and magazines.

A roach-strewn trestle table in the centre of the warehouse surrounded by a loose cluster of chairs and clouded in smoke, forms the hub and nerve centre of the Pollinator Company, where its founder and guiding spirit Mila Jansen – the undisputed marijuana matriarch of Amsterdam – holds court.

Mila is now in her late fifties and has devoted her life to pot. Short and stocky, with a pudding bowl fringe, Mila is delightfully scatterbrained as she bumbles around her warehouse, perennially puffing on enormous hash joints, a grin permanently plastered across her jolly face.

Her laugh is as chesty as her cough and at times it is difficult to tell the difference.

Mila was one of the early cannabis connoisseurs and helped pioneer the coffee shop scene in Amsterdam. As far back as 1967 – a full eight years before the first Bulldog coffee shop opened – Mila was running a tea house called Kink 22 where smoking spliffs was openly encouraged and was generally on the house. Although subsequently busted by the police and closed down, Kink 22 can justly claim to have been the prototype for the Amsterdam coffee shop scene that was to follow. After the Kink 22 bust, Mila decided to follow the hippie trail through Northern India, learning to hand press pollen and other impressive cannabis-related party tricks along the way.

She remembers those early days with nostalgia. 'I was smoking hash in Holland in the 1960s and then I lived in India for 14 years where they have very nice hash indeed. It was there, particularly around Manali, that I learnt how to hand rub my own hash and I also learnt how to use screens for sieving resin.

'Then I came back to Holland in the late 1980s and everyone was suddenly smoking this new grass. I didn't like that so much because I love my hash. So it just seemed kind of natural to keep making hash here. I started making my own over a flat screen and tumbling it.'

Right: A collection of bongs.

Cannabis convention

For all her hash consumption, Mila keeps herself very busy and always seems to be doing several things at the same time – deputising the production of a batch of hashish, greeting a friend, making a cup of tea, demonstrating a vaporiser pipe or politely explaining the niceties of a particularly arcane area of cannabis folklore to one of her constant stream of guests and visitors. A German grower swings by, keen for Mila to sample and assess the quality of his latest harvest. A young French girl hawking cannabis posters finds a sympathetic ear. A Japanese punk turns up wanting to buy a bong. An English hemp enthusiast wearing a porridgey hemp bobble hat earnestly discusses Scottish crop yields. Pot heads from all over the world pop in to pay their respects, each bringing the obligatory sticky lump of hash or bud of smelly sensi. All are made equally welcome and are sucked up into the lazy, hazy rhythm of the place.

But for all its shambolic air – the overflowing ashtrays, the endless succession of joints and pipes, the unattended lumps of hash the size of tennis balls – there is method in the apparent madness and all sorts of things are going on. On closer investigation, the warehouse with its numerous niches and antechambers reveals an Aladdin's cave of all things cannabis. The wooden shelves in its cavernous stock rooms are choc-a-bloc with hemp merchandise. Crates of cannabis champagne jostle for space with piles of hemp-woven clothes and stacks of propaganda. Every conceivable type of smoking paraphernalia is to be found here.

An indoor grow area to the rear of the warehouse is hung with metal halide lamps and houses a jungly thicket of mature plants adding to the general pleasant pong. There are also several trays of peyote cacti being cultivated with their distinctive mescaline buttons.

Mila is aided by her daughter Lali and an enthusiastic and cosmopolitan team of young assistants who help run the place as a sort of hippie cooperative. Lali helps out with all aspects of the business but her principal role is running the nearby Hemp Hotel where guests stay in cannabis-themed rooms, sleep beneath hemp blankets, wash with hemp soap, breakfast on hemp bread and hemp tea, drink hemp wines, beers and liqueur at the bar and keep the munchies at bay by snacking on dry roasted hemp seeds and hemp wine gums.

Mila's other loyal lieutenants include the dreadlocked Steven van den Veer. Steven acts as chief joint roller at the Pollinator Company – a

Left: Cannabis champagne. Right (clockwise from top): Pollen sieved through fine mesh; water extraction; hash left to dry.

full-time job often running into overtime. Glassy eyed and with a perennial grin plastered across his face, distracted does not even begin to describe Steven's absentmindedness. Prone to wandering off unexpectedly and in mid-sentence, as if heeding some inaudible calling, he will reappear equally mysteriously and unexpectedly half an hour later, languorously picking up the thread of conversation where he left off before conscientiously reapplying himself to his joint-rolling duties.

Then there is Robbie Terris – a mild-mannered Englishman who monitors Nederhash production in the aptly named wash room tucked away in a side recess of the warehouse. Mila's greatest achievement to date has undoubtedly been to pioneer Nederhash – a relatively new type of hashish made by extracting the THC-rich resin glands from sensimilla marijuana.

The idea first came to her while watching her laundry spinning round one day. She remembers, 'One day I was standing in front of my tumble-drier doing my laundry and I suddenly realised that what those clothes were doing in the drier I was recreating manually with all these leaves above a flat screen.'

She was intrigued by the way in which the specks of dirt were flushed out from the wash via holes pierced into the sides of the revolving chamber or drum.

Using the washing machine as her prototype, Mila went on to develop her revolutionary Ice-O-Lator system of resin extraction. The idea is beautifully simple. A gauze bag of marijuana is placed into a washing machine. The washing machine is pumped full of ice cold water, which promotes the crystallisation of the resin glands and stops them rupturing. Once the machine is turned on, these brittle glands are flushed through the mesh of the inner bag into a more closely knit outer bag, which then captures them. There they form into a fine sand-like blonde sludge or residue while the plant detritus remains trapped in the inner bag.

This resin powder is then scooped out of the outer bag and dried using a Dim Sum-style arrangement of stacked bamboo baskets through which air is pumped via a dehydrator.

Mila explains: 'You end up with pure THC resin crystals of much higher potency than usual. If you are lazy like me you just smoke them like that, otherwise you can press them into hash.'

Robbie prefers to press his pollen into proper hashish. 'By pressing the resin glands into hashish you can develop different flavours, especially with age,' he explains. 'It can be aged from six months up to ten years. There are a variety of ways of pressing, including bat pressing for which we use a rubber mallet to pound the glands between layers of cellophane, or plate pressing for which we have a hydraulic press that produces 50g slabs. The longer you press it, the

Clockwise from top left: The Ice-O-Lator system at the Pollinator Company relies on washing-machine technology; getting busy with a vaporiser pipe.

darker and the better it becomes as more resin glands are ruptured to release their oil. I often leave my hash in the plate press overnight or even for up to a couple of days.'

Ice-O-Lator revolution

Steve Hager, editor of pothead fanzine *High Times*, is a big fan. 'The Ice-O-Lator has really taken over the hash scene in Amsterdam,' he says. 'It used to be all about Nepalese and Moroccan but that has all changed now.'

What Mila and her ten-strong team of helpers at the Pollinator Company are producing is revolutionising the world of hashish. Mila remarks, 'There are as many different types of Nederhash as there are different types of sensi, but most of the coffee shops just give them generic names like Moonshine or Jelly at the Dampkring or Ice-O-Lator hash at other places. But if you go to the Bushdoctor, they list them under the names of the different grasses they actually come from in the first place, so you can get hash types like Orange Bud, Skunk or Northern Lights.'

Generally speaking, it is only the smaller buds and leaves that are used in the production of Nederhash. 'Because of the market demand for marijuana it makes more sense to use the big fat buds for marijuana,' Robbie explains. 'Nederhash is more of a by-product for which we use just the small buds and the side leaves surrounding the buds. Occasionally for fun we use the big buds too and this produces extremely potent and sticky hash. But, by and large,

it works out more economical to sell the big buds as marijuana.'

Do the Pollinator folk favour a particular types of grass when producing their Nederhash?

'A lot of it depends on the genetics of the different plants,' says Robbie. 'Some plants are more prolific and yield more crystals than others. There are a lot of variations in smell and taste and colour.

'But often we end up using the same varieties. We mainly use Northern Lights or White Widow. There is a huge demand at the moment for white marijuana that looks like it is frosted. There are only two or three of these types around and they all come from America. A lot of the growers are using them.

'Most of the hashish we make here is for the growers who bring their leaf material in after they have extracted the big buds. We tend to make it on a relatively small scale, not really enough to supply the coffee shops. Often the grower will only get about 50g back – only really enough for themselves.'

The Ice-O-Lator was developed from an earlier model called the Pollinator, which also used washing machine technology. Mila explains the subtle differences between the two systems. 'The pollen produced by the Pollinator was slightly less refined, and it didn't filter the crystal stems out like the Ice-O-Lator does. This means that the hash produced by the Pollinator system is tastier but has a lower THC content than the stuff coming from the Ice-O-Lator. Some people prefer one type to the other. Me, I don't mind either way,' she muses. 'It depends on my mood.'

Just as the sensimilla revolution of the 1970s and 1980s represented the appliance of science to marijuana cultivation, so Mila's development of Nederhash represents a parallel progression in the field of hashish production. Its coming has enabled us to produce as many different types of hash as there are different types of sensimilla. The potential is enormous and its impact is already being seen in Amsterdam's coffee shop trade. With many Dutch connoisseurs already owning their own Ice-O-Lators and almost 50 new ones being exported each month, all the signs suggest that Nederhash is going to be the next big trend in cannabis culture.

Seeds of change

Amsterdam's trade in cannabis seeds first started in the early 1980s. It has steadily grown since then and there are now about a dozen well-established businesses that specialise in retail, wholesale, mail order or a combination of the three.

One of the oldest and most highly regarded of the seed dealers is the family run Sensi Seed Bank. Ben Dronkers is its founder and guiding spirit. Dronkers looks much younger than his 52 years. He is blond with playboy good looks and habitually dresses in dark sober suits and open-neck shirts. He has a good head of glossy hair and an equally good set of flashing white teeth, in spite of his habit of chainsmoking hashish joints. Asked how he first became involved with the cannabis scene, he replies with a grin, 'I smoked a joint.'

Most of his six offspring have followed him into the business. 'Five of my six children smoke,' he says. 'And I'm happy with that. They don't drink. They don't take cocaine or ecstasy. They are regular people, they are not crazy people.'

Like many involved in Amsterdam's cannabis culture, Dronkers is fanatical in his devotion to dope. Apart from the core seed business he also runs a coffee shop under the same Sensi banner. He also founded the Hash Marijuana Hemp Museum, of which he is immensely proud, 15 years ago in the basement of his seed store. Indeed, such is his commitment to cannabis that he even christened one of his sensi strains after his twin daughters Shiva and Shanti.

He is an astute businessman, too, and the Sensi Seed Bank has grown dramatically since he founded the company more than 20 years ago. 'We are by far the biggest seed company,' he says. 'I have about 100 people working for me. We sell from (euros) 3 million to 4 million worth of seeds a year. And that's just the seeds. We also sell about (euros) 2.5 million in hemp products as well.

'About a third of our business is export but we don't export to countries where it is actually forbidden and we don't send seeds to countries we don't like – Sweden, for example. The Swedish government is the most crazy government in the world and the Swedish are the most alcoholic people in Europe.'

"Reefers [*are*] habit forming. All perverts may not be marijuana smokers, but practically all marijuana smokers are perverts"

Colonel Garland Williams, former Head of US Narcotics Enforcement

US influence

According to cult cannabis writer Robert Connell Clarke, certain key genetic elements were originally supplied to the early Amsterdam growers by American breeders in the form of seeds and cuttings. He says that this original genetic bank has since been continuously recycled. And he says that the appearance of new indigenous seeds on the scene to play around with are nowadays the exception rather than the rule.

He writes, 'Of the... varieties offered for sale by Dutch seed companies in 2000, 80 per cent of them contain germ plasm that first came to the Netherlands prior to 1985. Most of the seed companies have continued to shuffle the heavily stacked deck of original North American germ plasm, and since the 1980s few companies have introduced anything new.'

Of course a certain amount of genetic reshuffling is to be expected given that the strains that are commercially produced are generally done so for good reasons, such as their potency or flavour. So it is perhaps perfectly natural that the same core building blocks, notably Skunk Number One, crop up over and over again in the production of new commercial cultivars.

Clarke dissects this original plasm into eight distinct varieties, which he says were vested in several Dutch seed companies in the early 1980s and which each then went on to develop and hone them independently, occasionally developing new hybrids – such as Holland's Hope or Amstel

Gold – by introducing increasingly rare batches of indigenous seeds to their breeding programmes. Again, according to Clarke, as the Amsterdam seed companies proliferated in the 1990s, mainly feeding off the pioneering work done by the Americans in the 1970s and 1980s, the price of buying seeds dramatically rose.

However, Dronkers resents Clarke's suggestion that it was the North American growers who were exclusively responsible for creating the Dutch sensimilla scene in the early 1980s.

But he concedes that there was some input in terms of seeds and know-how. In particular he singles out for praise the contribution made by cultivation expert Ed Rosenthal – a former *High Times* columnist. 'Ed was involved in the Amsterdam sensi scene from the beginning. He came to see what we were doing in the greenhouses and wrote about it in *High Times* and in his famous books which went on to become bibles for growers all over the world.'

'The Americans were the first homegrowers, that is for sure. And they certainly smoke more marijuana than anyone else. Maybe that's because it's against the law,' he ponders, losing the thread and going off on one of his characteristic tangents. 'It is a curious fact that we have less cannabis smokers per capita here in Holland where it is allowed than you do in England, Denmark or France where it is forbidden.'

Right: American protesters get their message across with a witty banner.

Dronkers deplores the criminalisation of marijuana, especially in America, observing, 'Here in Holland you can have regular prescribed marijuana from your doctor if you have MS or AIDs. But in America they just lock their sick people up in prisons for possessing it. That can't be right.'

And he insists that the Dutch in general, and himself in particular, should take much of the credit for the pioneering genetic engineering that has taken place since sensi first appeared.

Dronkers estimates that there are now as many as 250 different seed strains on the market. And these represent by no means the end of the story. These 250 are just the stabilised marijuana strains that have been branded. There is virtually an infinite number of potential sensimilla types out there. Jason King – not the flamboyant 1970s TV star but the world's top pot photographer – recently featured 250 different types in his voluminous tome *The Cannabible*. And he readily confesses that the book is by no means exhaustive or encyclopaedic. He says he knows of at least 300 other types that he is still to cover in future editions.

Dronkers, for his part, insists that most of the seeds used to develop the Sensi Seed Bank's 25-strong stable of thoroughbred strains he personally sourced while travelling the hippie trail in the 1970s. And he is one of the very few Amsterdam seed dealers to have staked his claims by resort to copyright. He says, 'A lot of the quality breeding has been done in Holland.

Sensi Seeds exhibit at the Cannabis Cup.

True, some of the early seeds came from America. But when I started breeding I brought over Turkish varieties, Afghani varieties: varieties from all over the world.

'I had some experience of working in greenhouses in Holland and I learnt a lot from that and from people growing tomatoes and flowers.

'Then I started applying that greenhouse technology to growing cannabis indoors.'

The Sensi Seed Bank is clearly the biggest and best-established seed company in Amsterdam but that hasn't stopped quite a few sophisticated rivals from appearing on the scene over the last few years.

Clarke writes that, after a relatively long period of stagnation in the Dutch seed market that produced little but variation on the theme of the original American plasm, there have recently been promising signs of new life. He singles out several outdoor sativas from around Seattle – Blue Velvet, Flo and Blueberry – for particular praise. These are marketed in Amsterdam by the Sagarmatha and Dutch Passion seed companies. Clarke also rates two other strains introduced about 10 years ago – Bubblegum from Indiana and Sage from California. Both are marketed by the American owned TH Seeds Company, formerly known as the KGB and the CIA. It specialises in seeds sourced from America, and it emerged along with several other new seed companies in the early 1990s. One of its partners, New Yorker Adam Dunn, learnt the tricks of the trade while working for Dronkers at Sensi. Dunn, who sports a stylish crop and giant day-glo red plastic earrings, was personally responsible for launching the highly successful Bubblegum strain.

He says he first offered it to his former employers at Sensi but that they arrogantly turned it down, failing to recognise its potential. So he decided to go it alone. 'Me and my business partner thought there was too much Dutch stuff around so we introduced a whole load of new varieties from the States,' he says. 'I knew I was on to something special with Bubblegum. So we started breeding with it at TH Seeds and it was a great hit. Since then we have introduced quite a few new varieties like Snow Bud and Sage that have proved equally popular.'

And Adam sides with Clarke in thinking that early American breeders had more influence on the marijuana scene in Amsterdam than Dronkers gives them credit for. 'Before the Americans brought over Skunk Number One and those other early sensis in the early 1980s, the Europeans were mainly smoking imported hash. Back then they couldn't really tell the difference between hemp and real weed.

'It was the American Sacred Seed Company that originally brought the genetics over to Amsterdam in the early 1980s. They were more into research than actually selling the stuff. The Americans brought over both Skunk Number One and Haze. Then they split and the Dutch started working from there. Sure,' he admits, 'the Dutch have since clocked up a very respectable 25 years of growing experience. But just because cannabis growing in Amsterdam is flourishing doesn't mean that cannabis culture is dead in the States. Far from it. In fact it is still

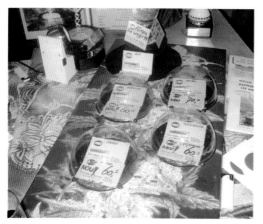

Above: Seed varieties on display at the Cup.

very much alive. It just has to be done with a lot more secrecy there than in Amsterdam because of the law. In Amsterdam it is a lot more open but it is also a lot more commercial.

'But the American harvest festivals are still very big, especially in Northern California. And the emphasis there is much more on the weed and less on the trade than it is, say, at Amsterdam's Cannabis Cup. Canada also has big harvest festivals too.'

However, when all is said and done, whoever deserves the credit for pioneering Dutch sensi – whether it was the Americans or the Dutch – it doesn't make that much difference in the grand scheme of things. Spenser, a young English grower with the Flying Dutchman Seed

Company, puts it in perspective, 'These plants have been on the planet long before the breeders ever made their selections 25 years ago. OK, granted the original Skunk Number One was and continues to be one of the best strains for breeding. Granted, too, that it was originally put together in America. But one shouldn't forget that Skunk Number One is a cocktail of strains originating in Mexico, Thailand and Colombia. So none of it is really the property of anybody. It doesn't belong to any nation in particular. It belongs to the world.'

The question of who kickstarted the sensi scene in Amsterdam aside, breeding cannabis is undoubtedly a highly skilled and painstaking process. Consistency of results is what the growers are after – a more or less uniform quality of yield and potency – and the more reputable of the Dutch breeders take great pride in providing their customers with complete pedigrees for their wares. So only those cultivars that have been sufficiently skilfully genetically engineered by breeders end up dominating the market, while seeds that have been produced less scientifically and fail to deliver consistent results fall by the wayside.

Broadly speaking, stabilisation in seed performance is best achieved by repeatedly inbreeding a batch of cuttings of known parentage over a number of generations so that the desired traits become indelibly printed within the resulting seeds. The seeds need to be stabilised into what are known as F1s. F1s are produced by selectively interbreeding seeds

'Skunk Number One is a cocktail of strains originating in Mexico, Thailand and Colombia"

which are of known parentage over five generations – a process which can involve up to 20,000 plants and take up to four years to perfect. However, it is worth the effort because these fabulous F1 seeds will then produce plants of consistent quality – a factor high on the grower's list of priorities.

Less reputable seed dealers tend to fob off growers with non-stabilised seeds, the progeny of which can be extremely unpredictable.

'There is still room out there for good new seed companies,' Dronkers concedes.
'But unfortunately 98 per cent of them are phonies producing non-stabilised seeds.'

Dronkers reckons that there are around 250 different varieties of stabilised seeds on the market at the moment – around a tenth of them owned by Sensi itself. And he acknowledges that the potential for recrossing those 250 seeds to produce new stabilised hybrids is virtually endless. But he sees the recent ban on indoor cultivation as a definite hindrance to breeders. 'Breeding is becoming more secretive because of the new tighter legislation,' he says. 'We are of course still breeding but on a much smaller scale compared to before.'

Apart from regular stabilised seeds, new 'feminised' seeds have been appearing in Amsterdam over the last few years. They cost twice as much as regular ones but their promoters say that they are virtually guaranteed to produce only female plants, thus obviating the need to weed out the males – a process that wastes space and slows down the growing cycle. Feminised seeds were pioneered in the early 1990s by Henk van Dalen, owner of the Dutch Passion Seed Company, which has developed 20 different strains of them. 'Our first method of producing feminised seeds was from female plants which had been isolated from male plants and were close to the end of their flowering. Sometimes these females would develop hermaphrodite qualities in the form of pseudo-male flowers near the end of their growth cycles. If you allow self-pollination to take place under these conditions, the resulting seeds will be feminised, meaning they will almost invariably produce only female plants.

"I'm 52 and I've been smoking cannabis every day for 35 years"

Free samples are on offer at most stands.

'If grown indoors by experienced growers and under stable conditions then you will have 100 per cent guaranteed female plants, although outdoor conditions are more variable and less easy to control.' Henk says his feminised seeds are proving very popular and that his sales of them recently outstripped sales of regular seeds for the first time.

But the jury is still out on feminised seeds and Dronkers for one is unconvinced. 'Sensi doesn't produce feminised seeds because I believe in nature. They are not 100 per cent guaranteed and, as things stand, I think that growing a mixed garden and then taking clones from the females is still probably the best and most reliable system available to growers.' Tighter legislation and feminised seeds apart, Dronkers is optimistic regarding the future of the cannabis scene in Amsterdam. He bullishly predicts strong growth in both the coffee shop and the seed sectors. And, like his friend Jack Herer – whom he has honoured by naming one of his cannabis strains after him – he sees a big future in hemp. 'I have known and respected Jack for almost 20 years,' he says. 'But I first started looking to get involved in the hemp market myself about eight years ago.

'Today I own 2,000 hectares (around 8 square miles) of hemp, mainly in Holland but also some over the border in Germany.

'I've got 100 farmers working for me and we just make raw hemp, cultivating it for the fibre. I really believe that Jack is right – that hemp is the plant that can save the world. It is not just a dream. It is a matter of fact.

The Sensi Seeds stand at the Cannabis Cup.

'Show me one other crop that doesn't need insecticides or pesticides. Show me one.

'And also there is no waste. We use the whole thing, right down to the roots.'

'And with the new hemp business we are exporting about 7,000 tons a year in total – quite a lot to Germany and also to Eastern Europe.

'But we export the most of all to Turkey. We sold about 3,000 tons last year to the Turks – that's 150 truckloads.'

Dronkers pauses to take a toke before embarking on another of his trademark detours. 'That's quite ironic because, unlike in the past, nowadays it is virtually impossible to find any decent hash in Turkey. It is totally forbidden. There's lots of heroin but no hash. And you know what they do with that hemp of ours that

they import? They smoke it. They make cigarette papers out of it and smoke it. Isn't that funny?'

Dronkers prepares to skin up his umpteenth joint of the day. They are beginning to take their toll. His expression is becoming glassy, his speech slurred and his mind is wandering again. He's becoming prone to increasingly wild flights of the imagination. He likens the city's cannabis culture of today to the Dutch Golden Age of the 17th century. 'Back then,' he croaks dreamily, 'traders from Amsterdam made vast fortunes dealing in spices and tobacco which they bought back from the East. They created the wealth and culture of Holland's Golden Age – our great painters, like Rembrandt.

'I think today their place has been taken by the cannabis traders – the seed dealers and the coffee shop owners – who have created this new prosperous business and culture in Amsterdam.'

He loses the plot. A cloud furrows his brow and his mood changes. 'I'm 52 and I've been smoking cannabis every day for 35 years. For all that time the politicians and the policemen have been saying it should be forbidden. Why? Was alcohol prohibition good in the United States? No it wasn't. We got the Mafia from it. And it is the same story with every type of prohibition.

'When I was a kid starting to smoke, we were smoking marijuana from Africa and South America. That was coming from monsters like Idi Amin in Africa or from Colombian drug barons. The dictators, the gangsters and the criminals were supplying that cannabis to the West – just like they are still doing with all their cocaine.'

Dronkers takes a final toke. 'Then I started to sell these fabulous seeds in Amsterdam and now all these people in Europe and America are growing their own marijuana instead of buying it from terrorists and criminals. 'I think I should be decorated. I deserve a medal.'

Cup fever

Apart from the coffee shops, the hashish manufacturers and the seed dealers, Amsterdam is also the venue for the Cannabis Cup of the Year – a five-day extravaganza organised by the American stoner magazine *High Times*.

High Times regards itself as the official voice of the counterculture, but is in fact more reminiscent of *Playboy* circa 1975 with its scantily clad cover girls and its lurid centrefold close-ups of sensimilla buds.

Editor Steven Hager, with a Bob Dylan bouffant and dressed head-to-toe in denim, tries to explain the thinking behind the magazine and the event it organises. 'We represent the counterculture which is really like a baby infant spirituality that was born in New Orleans where native Americans, blacks and whites came together to party and jam. The idea of all cultures accepting each other and coming together in harmony first came about there. And that is what the counterculture is all about – no barriers with all tribes united together and for peace.'

He is building up steam. 'All the problems, all the wars, all the anxiety, all the terror are the fault of religious fundamentalism, the idea that one person has a monopoly on access to god. We don't believe that. We believe everybody has got direct line access right in their hearts to god, that it's written into them. We also believe that cannabis can help you hook up with that access if it is used in a responsible matter.

'We're like one family. We all love each other and we all come together to do the cup in Amsterdam every year. Nobody is trying to engineer anything. It just doesn't have that vibration,' he concludes mysteriously.

Such sub-Woodstock sentiments don't carry much weight with one veteran American cupper who comments, '*High Times* is run by a very strange group of New Yorkers. They are stoners but at the same time they're on this very heavy mystic trip. They are entitled to their opinions but I don't really want to hear about all this cult shit. There have even been a couple of cups where they wanted everybody to hold hands and make a circle.'

He shakes his head and frowns, 'It's just so low budget. They really have to get up to speed, get more with it and a bit more MTV slick. The problem is they want to spend two grand and make fifty instead of spending fifty grand and making a million.'

High Times takes charge

Hager claims credit for inaugurating the Cannabis Cup in 1987 and recently awarded himself an award in recognition of this achievement. However, seasoned cup-goers

"One stand is promoting a thermostatically-controlled grow room camou-flaged as an office filing cabinet"

challenge this official line, citing the author and horticulturalist Ed Rosenthal as the true founder. Rosenthal is said to have staged the first cup with a budget of just $600, but with buckets of goodwill from his many friends in Amsterdam. Back then the cup was less of a money spinner and more of a party – an excuse for a bunch of fellow potheads to get blitzed once a year in Amsterdam during the traditionally slack Thanksgiving period. It was only later, these critics argue, that *High Times* latched on to the profit potential and effectively hijacked it for commercial purposes.

Be that as it may, Rosenthal has since been banished from the inner circle of *High Times* and the cup has become a regular fixture in the cannabis calendar, regularly attracting several thousand people to the city in late November. They come from all over the world but the vast majority are young American men who spend up to US$2,000 for all-in packages to the event.

Delegates, visitors and B-list celebrity panels of judges – a recent 'star' guest was Joan Baez's brother – cast their votes in more than half-a-dozen categories including best marijuana, best hash, best seed dealer and best coffee shop. Winners stand to enjoy considerable publicity, so competition can be fierce. However, the initial selection procedure seems to be a fairly arbitrary process carried out by the *High Times* editorial team, and one is left wondering whether the whole thing amounts to much more than a lucrative and self-serving exercise in public relations for all concerned.

The Cup's HQ is the Pax Party House – a three-storey building on the outskirts of the city near the Heineken Brewery, cheekily sited next door to a police station. Security is provided by enormous black guys dressed in gangsta gear and chunky gold jewellery. Lectures and seminars – mainly conducted by Hager and his

Cannabis Cup trophies, including the giant Sweetleaf grinder.

team of cannabis cronies – run throughout the day on the ground floor. The people might be high but the level of debate is not and what little entertainment is provided is mostly of the infantile joint-smoking competition variety.

Meanwhile, the upper two floors are given over to a trade fair. This is very much like any other trade fair apart from the freebies – joints and blasts on bongs rather than key rings and ballpoint pens. All the major seed dealers and quite a few of the coffee shops have stands there, as do a bewildering variety of international manufacturers and wholesalers: bong manufacturers from Detroit, underground comic publishers from San Francisco, hemp clothing specialists from Switzerland, grow room specialists from Germany, grass grinder producers from Canada. Other stalls hawk sieving devices and honey oil-making kits. One stand is promoting a thermostatically controlled grow room camouflaged as an office filing cabinet, while yet another is plugging a device called the Urinator – an electronic gizmo designed to foil drug testing, which comes supplied with sachets of toxin-free dehydrated piss. Yet another is touting a product called Knotty Boy – a hair-care solution designed to help with dreadlocks.

The air is so thick with smoke that one can barely see across the room and every other stallholder is offering free hits on some Heath Robinson pipe or other.

There are half a dozen different types of vaporiser pipes alone, some involving oxygen-style masks, while one stand is promoting the Atom Bong – an ingenious water pipe involving a sliding glass periscope action.

'Wanna vaporise?' barks a blank-faced young girl in cheerleader outfit to the passing procession of zonked-out kids. The enigmatic Soma of Soma Seeds sits behind his stand, giant bong at hand. Flanked by two lighter-wielding handmaidens, he has a fixed grin on his face, his gold teeth glittering through the constant smog of smoke, his long grizzled locks coiled, Shiva like, on his gaunt head into a bird's-nest bun. Across the room a bevy of bikini-clad beauties disport themselves in an inflatable paddling pool while blowing bubbles through plastic rings and toking on joints.

A fleet of minibuses wait outside the Pax Party House to whisk delegates off on tours of the city's various competing coffee shops – up to 30 of them, which means ten a day for conscientious, but no doubt barely conscious, visiting delegates – where yet more freebies are on offer.

For those still standing, the action shifts to the cavernous Milkyway nightclub in the evening, where the free hits on bongs and vaporisers continue. Bands and lightshows are laid on but the dancing is desultory as double vision sets in.

The paying punters are mostly college boys with oversized wallets and undersized imaginations – pot anoraks and Neanderthal numbskulls dressed in baggy romper suits and baseball caps.

As they are shunted around the participating coffee shops in cavalcades of clapped-out minibuses appallingly driven by even more clapped-out drivers they seem to see the city as a kind of cannabis theme park. The locals regard these invading hordes of overweight, dreadlocked and body-pierced young men with ambivalence – deploring their gaucheness and vulgarity but at the same time welcoming their steady flow of Euros at this traditionally off-peak and slack time of year. As one jaded local man puts it, 'I feel sorry for these guys who come over here for the Cup. They are living in la-la land. They don't really get a chance to see Amsterdam as it really is.

'It certainly isn't like this the rest of the year,' he confides. 'This week everyone is giving away books, giving away dope, giving away T-shirts, giving away everything. But for the rest of the year the Dutch are cheap as hell – they don't give away anything.'

The coffee shops themselves pay for the privilege of entering into the cup. And many of them additionally lay on free spliff in a bid to win votes. One can only assume that the resulting publicity – mainly trumpeted through the pages of *High Times* and other headzines – justifies the expenditure.

By the time the final votes are counted, the smoke is beginning to take its toll. Signs of physical and mental deterioration are becoming increasingly apparent. Delegates shuffle around unseeing, overwhelmed by the sheer volume of smoke. Bloodshot eyes are blank and smarting, eyelids glued together, feet unsteady, memory faltering, dreams dissolving, hallucinations setting in. Coughs shift register from chesty to guttural and voices have been reduced to pathetic croaks. Paranoia and cannabis psychosis is endemic. Focusing, let alone judging, is becoming a problem.

Basil Bush

A lanky white rastafarian emerges like a genie from the smoke. Slit eyes peer through rubber eyelids and John Lennon specs. A wispy beard frames a fixed grin on a pallid face, while heavy dreadlocks hang down to the waist. This is the legendary Basil Bush – arguably England's leading purveyor of bongs and other smoking paraphernalia.

He hasn't bothered booking a stand at this year's cup but has just popped over for a couple of days' networking. Apart from his extensive wholesaling activities, Basil also fields his own

"A lanky white rasta emerges like a genie from the smoke ... this is the legendary Basil Bush"

brand of mesh hash pipe filters – long regarded as the industry standard in the UK. He has also recently diversified into kingsize rolling papers – bearing both his own distinctive features and the motto 'toking since long time'. His latest bright idea is to develop a camouflaged line of papers especially for smoking in the country or on those occasions when discretion is called for.

Although the paraphernalia he deals in is clearly tailor made for cannabis consumption, Basil stubbornly plays down that side of his business. He insists that tobacconists, not headshops, account for by far the biggest chunk of his business; that his pipes, bongs and papers are intended exclusively for smoking tobacco; and that the cannabis seeds he has recently started dealing in are sold simply as 'souvenirs' rather than for the purposes of illegal germination.

He first stumbled into the bong business at the height of Thatcherism in the mid-1980s. He was out of work at the time and decided to try his luck applying for a government initiative called the Enterprise Allowance scheme, which was aimed at reducing unemployment figures by giving people small sums of cash to help start up their own businesses. It didn't add up to much more money than regular benefit, but at least it meant he could skip the ritual of signing on for six months. He recalls: 'OK, even back then £40 a week in England wasn't much but you could live like a king in India on that. So I buggered off to the Himalayas for six months, where I smoked it up righteous.

'When the six months was up I thought, well man, I've got to have something to show for all this, so I scored a load of chillums and pipes to take back home.'

Back in England, Basil hawked his merchandise around Glastonbury and the festival circuit. To his amazement he turned a tidy profit – the margins were, and remain, enormous. 'So, I thought, alright man, I better do another run...

'I've never looked back. The next thing I know it's 15 years later and I've got my picture splashed all over these packets of skins just like Ben and Jerry on their ice cream tubs. It's amazing.

'But the biggest buzz of all,' he grins, 'is that my success was all thanks to Thatch and her Enterprise Allowance Scheme. Nice one Maggie.'

Chapter 6

The Munchies

"Running around
Robbing banks
All whacked off
On Scooby Snacks"

Fun Lovin' Criminals

The Munchies

Smoking pot is renowned for stimulating the appetite and bringing on attacks of the munchies. By happy coincidence, these cravings offer dedicated potheads a further opportunity for consuming cannabis – by cooking it up in various tasty recipes.

However, when cooking with cannabis, certain provisos should be borne in mind. Firstly, the effects of eating it are not as instantaneous or as quantifiable as when smoking it. It takes longer to come on than smoking – sometimes up to a couple of hours. And when it does finally arrive, the effect is going to be a good deal stronger and longer. Often the effects of eating can last for up to 12 hours and will keep coming back in waves. Some find this experience scary and overwhelming. They say they feel more comfortable and in control of the situation when they smoke it.

And, of course, it goes without saying that it is totally out of order to ever spike anyone's food with dope without first obtaining their express consent. If, however, in spite of all this, you do decide to go ahead and give cooking with cannabis a go, at least be sure to err on the side of caution and keep individual intakes down to no more than a gram of hash or a couple of grams of grass per sitting.

Majoon

Pot is particularly suitable for use in sweet recipes and those involving lashings of chocolate. This has long been recognised. The ancient Arabs and Persians were particularly fond of using it to make majoon – an Arab word meaning sweetmeats laced with cannabis. A typical majoon might take the form of Turkish delight. Common ingredients used in making majoon confections included sugar, milk, cocoa butter, honey, crushed nuts and dried fruits.

The 19th-century potheads of Europe and America also chose to eat, rather than smoke, cannabis and would frequently employ sweetened preparations to mask its flavour. Cannabis featured in various medical tinctures of the time too – its psychoactive THC content being extracted by soaking it in alcohol.

One of the many common misconceptions about cannabis is that its psychoactive THC component can be extracted by boiling it in water. This is not the case. In fact, its THC content can only be extracted by using fats, oils or alcohol.

Each of the following recipes uses cannabis in its raw and natural state, prepared in conjunction with various fats and oils. However, for those intending to cook with cannabis on a regular basis it will probably make more sense to make up a batch of cannabis-laced 'space butter' to dip into whenever the occasion arises.

Space butter

To make 500g (1lb) of space butter, melt 500g (1lb) of regular butter in a saucepan and then gradually add 25g (1oz) of ground prime bud or hashish crumbs, or twice that amount of ground leaves. Stir continuously on a gentle heat for about half an hour. Pour the butter through a gauze strainer into jars, which should then be sealed and refrigerated.

The residual sludge left over can be used in smoothies, although its THC content will by now be fairly negligible having been transferred into the space butter. Then, whenever a recipe calls for conventional butter, simply replace with the space butter. Bon appetit!

Chocolate nut space fudge

The *Alice B Toklas Cook Book* of 1954 scandalised readers by including a recipe for hashish fudge, which she dubbed the 'food of paradise'. Toklas invented this recipe with the help of her long-time literary girlfriend Gertrude Stein and described the effects of eating it as including 'euphoria and brilliant storms of laughter, ecstatic reveries and extensions of one's personality'. The following is a variation on Toklas's original recipe.

125G (4OZ/1 STICK) UNSALTED BUTTER
4TBSPS BLACK COFFEE
2TBSPS COCOA POWDER
2TBSPS GOLDEN SYRUP
625G (1¼LB/5CUPS) CASTER SUGAR
20G (¾OZ) CRUMBLED HASH OR 40G (1½OZ) GROUND BUDS
200ML (7FL OZ) CONDENSED MILK
125G (4OZ/1 CUP) CHOPPED PECAN NUTS

1. Grease an 18 x 28cm baking tin.
2. Melt butter in a large pan and gradually stir in the hash or grass. Then add coffee, cocoa, syrup and sugar. Heat gently, stirring occasionally until the sugar has dissolved. Do not allow to boil at this stage or the finished fudge will crystallise and lack the desired smooth texture.
3. Add the condensed milk and bring to the boil, stirring. Boil steadily for 5 to 10 minutes, until the bubbles become more volcanic.
4. Turn off the heat and wait until the bubbling subsides. Then whisk briskly for about 5 minutes until the mixture becomes smoother and more glutinous.
5. Add the chopped nuts and mix them in well. Pour the mix onto the prepared baking tin and leave for 30 minutes until semi-set. Mark into 2.5cm squares with a sharp knife and then leave to fully chill and set.
6. Finally, cut into squares and store in a cool place in biscuit tins.

Magic mocha brownies

The hash brownie is a classic cannabis recipe. It's a great comfort food in winter and also comes into its own as an energy booster on activity holidays. Pack some in your emergency supplies when you're off on a hiking weekend. Chomp your way through a couple of these at base camp and you'll feel capable of taking on Everest. Hang on a minute, maybe toking on Everest would be a better idea…

125G (4OZ) DARK CHOCOLATE

50G (2OZ/½ STICK) UNSALTED BUTTER

14G (½OZ) CRUMBLED HASH OR 27G (1OZ) FINELY GROUND BUD

175G (6OZ/1CUP) DARK, SOFT, BROWN SUGAR

2 EGGS

1TBSPN STRONG BLACK COFFEE (COLD)

125G (4OZ/1 CUP) PLAIN FLOUR

½TSP BAKING POWDER

PINCH OF SALT

50G (2OZ/½ CUP) CHOPPED WALNUTS, PECANS OR BRAZIL NUTS

MAKES 16 BROWNIES

1. Preheat oven to 180°C/350°F/Gas 4. Grease and line a 20.5cm square cake tin.
2. Melt the chocolate, butter and hash or grass in a large pan over low heat, then set aside to cool down.
3. Beat the sugar and eggs together in a deep bowl until thick and pale. Fold in the melted chocolate mix and the cold coffee. Mix thoroughly. Sift in flour, baking powder and salt. Lightly fold into mixture. Then add the chopped nuts.
4. Pour the mixture into your prepared tin and bake in the oven for 25 to 30 minutes. Your Magic Mocha Brownies are done when firm and when an inserted fork comes out clean. Leave them to semi-cool for 30 minutes before cutting into squares. Store the brownies in a cool, dry place.

Sleepy-head hot chocolate

Sleepy-head hot chocolate is a godsend on those bitterly cold winter nights when you long for nothing more than to forget all your troubles and snuggle up under the duvet with a good book and a soothing hot drink. This delicious recipe blends the very best dark chocolate with the finest hashish in a delicious spaced-out combo. A steaming cup of this at bedtime is guaranteed to spread a delightful languor through tired limbs and infuse your inner self with a sense of well-being.
You'll be nodding off in no time. Sweet dreams.

50G (2OZ) GOOD QUALITY DARK CHOCOLATE SUCH AS VALRHONA MANJARI
2G (¹⁄₁₆OZ) GOOD QUALITY HASH, PREFERABLY BLACK
50ML (2FL OZ) SINGLE CREAM
300ML (2FL OZ) FULL-FAT MILK

TO SERVE:
WHIPPED CREAM
GRATED CHOCOLATE

ENOUGH FOR TWO CUPS

1. Break up the chocolate into small pieces. Heat the hash with a flame and crumble into smallest pieces possible, as if making a joint. Put the chocolate, hash and cream into a pan and stir under a medium heat until it melts.

2. Meanwhile, bring the milk to the boil in another saucepan and then pour over the melted chocolate. Briskly whisk for a while to stop a skin forming. Serve with whipped cream and grated chocolate.

Scooby snacks

Named after the cartoon canine hero Scooby Doo of the naff 1970s TV show. Why? Because scooby rhymes with doobie. And with delicious surprise-packed snacks like these around it's really no wonder that he always had the munchies and we couldn't understand a word he was saying. Scooby Snacks are quick, easy and straightforward to rustle up. Just blend together the ingredients, pop into the oven and in no time at all you'll be barking up the wrong tree. Where are you?

125G (4OZ/1STICK) UNSALTED BUTTER
50G (2OZ/5TBSP) GRANULATED SUGAR
50G (2OZ) LIGHT SOFT BROWN SUGAR
15G (½OZ) CRUMBLED HASH OR 30G (1OZ) GROUND GANJA
1 EGG
FEW DROPS VANILLA ESSENCE
125G (4OZ/1CUP) PLAIN FLOUR
15G (½OZ) COCOA POWDER
½TSP BICARBONATE OF SODA
125G (4OZ/⅔CUP) PLAIN DARK CHOCOLATE CHIPS
50G (2OZ/½CUP) ROUGHLY CHOPPED PECAN NUTS

MAKES ABOUT 30

1. Preheat oven to 180°C/350°F/Gas 4. Grease 3 baking sheets.
2. Cream the butter, sugars and cannabis in a bowl until light and fluffy. Meanwhile, in another bowl beat the egg and vanilla essence together. Gradually beat the egg mix into the butter mix.
3. Next sift the flour, cocoa and bicarbonate of soda over the creamed mixture, stirring it in carefully. Finally, add the choc chips and nuts.
4. Transfer teaspoon-sized dollops of the mixture onto the pre-prepared baking sheets, spacing the dollops well apart. Then bake in the oven for about 15 minutes until the mixture has spread out and the cookies are beginning to feel firm.
5. Remove from the oven and place on wire racks to cool and crisp. Store the Scooby Snacks in an airtight container somewhere dark and cool.

Mellow yellow ice cream

One of the best ways to consume pot and satisfy your munchies at the same time is to eat it as ice cream. Gently heating cannabis with cream is an extremely efficient way of maximising the extraction of the psychoactive THC component of cannabis. And storing the ice cream in the freezer will maintain its potency for many months to come. However, to get the best results, you should really use hash rather than grass in this recipe.

A nutritious and delicious dessert to roll out on those long, lazy summer afternoons lounging around in the garden.

25G (2TBSPNS/¼STICK) BUTTER
575ML (18FL OZ) SINGLE CREAM
75G (3OZ/3TBSPNS) SUGAR
PINCH SALT
7G (¼OZ) CRUMBLED HASH
450G (15OZ) BANANAS
3TBSPNS RUM
5TBSPNS HONEY
1/4 CUP CHOPPED WALNUTS

SERVES 6

1. Heat the cream in a saucepan until nearly boiling. In a second saucepan melt the butter with the sugar and salt. Heat the hash with a flame and crumble it into the melted butter, stirring all the while. Then whisk in the cream with the butter.
2. Peel bananas. Put them into a large bowl and mash with fork. Add the cream, rum, honey and walnuts. Beat well to mix. Pour mixture into a chilled shallow plastic container. Cover and freeze for a couple of hours until mixture is mushy in consistency. Turn out mixture into a chilled bowl. Beat with a metal fork or whisk until smooth.
3. Return mixture to container, cover and freeze until firm. Transfer to the refrigerator 30 minutes before serving to soften. Serve in scoops in individual glasses with cookies.

Potty pizza

Although traditionally consumed in sweet dishes and desserts, cannabis can also be used to spice up savoury dishes. Pizza is in many ways an ideal candidate, the hash or grass blending in well with the other earthy flavours. The following provides just a basic recipe which can be embellished with further pizza toppings according to taste.

FOR THE DOUGH:

400G (13OZ/3½CUPS) PLAIN FLOUR
25G (1OZ) YEAST
1TSP SUGAR
250ML (8FL OZ) WARM WATER
1TSP SALT
2TBSPS OLIVE OIL

FOR THE TOPPING:
OLIVE OIL FOR FRYING
1 LARGE ONION, FINELY SLICED
1 LARGE RED PEPPER
8G FINELY CRUMBLED HASH OR 16G GROUND BUD
175G (6OZ) FINELY SLICED MUSHROOMS
1 CAN OF PLUM TOMATOES, DRAINED AND FINELY CHOPPED
250G (8OZ/2CUPS) GRATED SWISS OR ITALIAN CHEESE
12 STONED OLIVES
OLIVE OIL

MAKES TWO LARGE PIZZAS

1. To make the dough, sift the flour into a bowl. Scoop out a well in the centre and crumble in the yeast and sugar. Then add the water, knead into a heavy dough, cover with a cloth and leave in a warm place to rise for 30 minutes. Then add the salt and oil. Beat into a smooth paste with a wooden spoon. Knead into a ball, coat with flour and set to one side.
2. For the topping, gently fry red pepper and onion in oil. Gradually add in the sliced mushrooms and the hash or grass. Gently cook for 5 to 10 minutes.
3. Roll out the pizza dough into two circular bases. Spread the tomatoes over the dough and then add the onion and mushroom topping. Sprinkle with olives and grated cheese. Grill or bake in a hot oven for around 10 minutes.

Chapter 7

Smoke Signals

"Dope will be legalised in a few years.
Even the lawyers are smoking it."

Lenny Bruce

Smoke Signals

There is a growing recognition that sooner or later cannabis is going to be legalised. One significant factor in its rehabilitation has been the increasingly vociferous and well-organised efforts of campaigning activists.

Groups like the National Organization for the Reform of Marijuana Laws (NORML) in the US have worked tirelessly 'to move public opinion sufficiently to achieve the repeal of marijuana prohibition so that the responsible use of cannabis by adults is no longer subject to penalty.' NORML boasts grassroots support across 37 American states, with overseas branches as far afield as Jamaica, Israel and New Zealand.

Pot panacea

One of the most persuasive arguments in the campaign to get cannabis legalised has been the medical one. Although the ancient Chinese, Romans and Scythians were well aware of the plant's healing properties, interest in this aspect of cannabis has only relatively recently revived in the West.

However, a raft of research conducted over the last few years suggests that pot could prove a positive panacea in the treatment of a number of serious medical conditions. One of these is glaucoma – an eye complaint that can lead to progressive vision loss and even blindness. Cannabis can help relieve the symptoms of glaucoma by reducing internal eye pressure. Pot-smoking is also a great expectorant and has been used to treat symptoms of lung congestion brought on by both asthma and emphysema.

Cannabis is also an excellent appetite stimulant and has proved remarkably effective in helping patients suffering from the nausea or lack of appetite that is associated with chemotherapy, AIDs and anorexia.

Its analgesic properties, too, have been deployed to treat a wide variety of complaints, including migraine, rheumatism and arthritis, while its capacity to control tremors and spasms makes it an ideal medicine for treating epilepsy and multiple sclerosis.

Right: A California State Medication License.

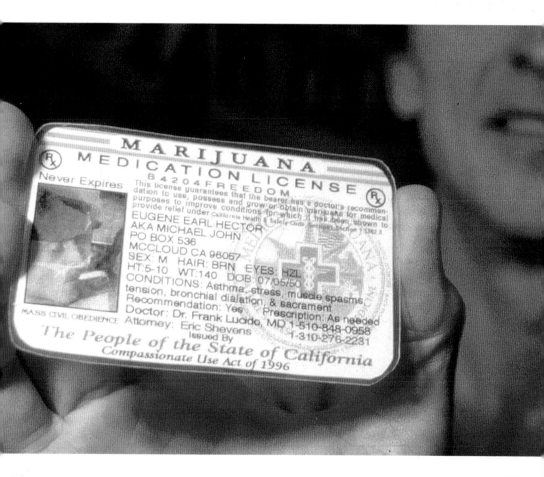

Nor are its medical applications restricted to only physical symptoms. Recreational smokers have long recognised and cherished the calming qualities of cannabis – the psychoactive 'high' that lifts the spirits. Psychiatrists finally latched onto this feelgood factor in the late 1980s when a series of research projects revealed that a THC-like chemical is spontaneously produced in the brains of mammals to act as a natural stress-busting agent. They christened this chemical anandamide, from 'ananda' – the Sanskrit word for bliss. And they discovered that supplementing this internal bank of THC with cannabis top-ups could often work wonders when treating patients suffering from depression.

Pot perils

Of course, dope is not without its detractors. While forced by the weight of evidence to concede that cannabis is not actually physically addictive, some critics of the drug claim that prolonged use can, nevertheless, lead to a form of psychological dependency – a charge that could equally well be levelled at substances as innocuous as chewing gum or chocolate.

A steamy solution to carcinogens

Then there is the thorny question of carcinogens. A recent report by the British Lung Foundation called 'A Smoking Gun?' claimed cannabis has 50 per cent more cancer-inducing carcinogens than tobacco. Moreover, some experts say that this high level of carcinogens combined with the tendency for cannabis smokers to prolong inhalation for as long as possible in order to achieve the optimum hit can result in 'vanishing lung syndrome', a condition in which the lungs' air sacs become obstructed by cysts and breathing becomes problematic.

Although carcinogens and vanishing lung syndrome are both causes for concern, such risks can be reduced or even totally avoided by the obvious expedient of changing the mode of cannabis consumption. Most of the carcinogens, tar and carbon monoxide can be filtered out of the smoke by using a water pipe or, even more effectively, by opting for a vaporizer. With a vaporizer you inhale a steam vapour rather than carcinogen-clogged smoke. And additional bonuses of the vaporizer are that it is less wasteful, more flavoursome and delivers a consistently higher THC hit to the toker than does conventional smoke; hardly surprising, then, that vaporizers are becoming increasingly popular among both recreational and medical cannabis users. Another carcinogen-free option is eating or drinking. Cannabis lends itself well to consumption in a wide range of foods and tinctures thanks to the fact that its psychoactive THC content is soluble in both fats and alcohol.

Right: A medical marijuana supporter hangs her head after marijuana guru Ed Rosenthal is convicted by a federal jury of three counts of marijuana cultivation and conspiracy in San Francisco in 2003.

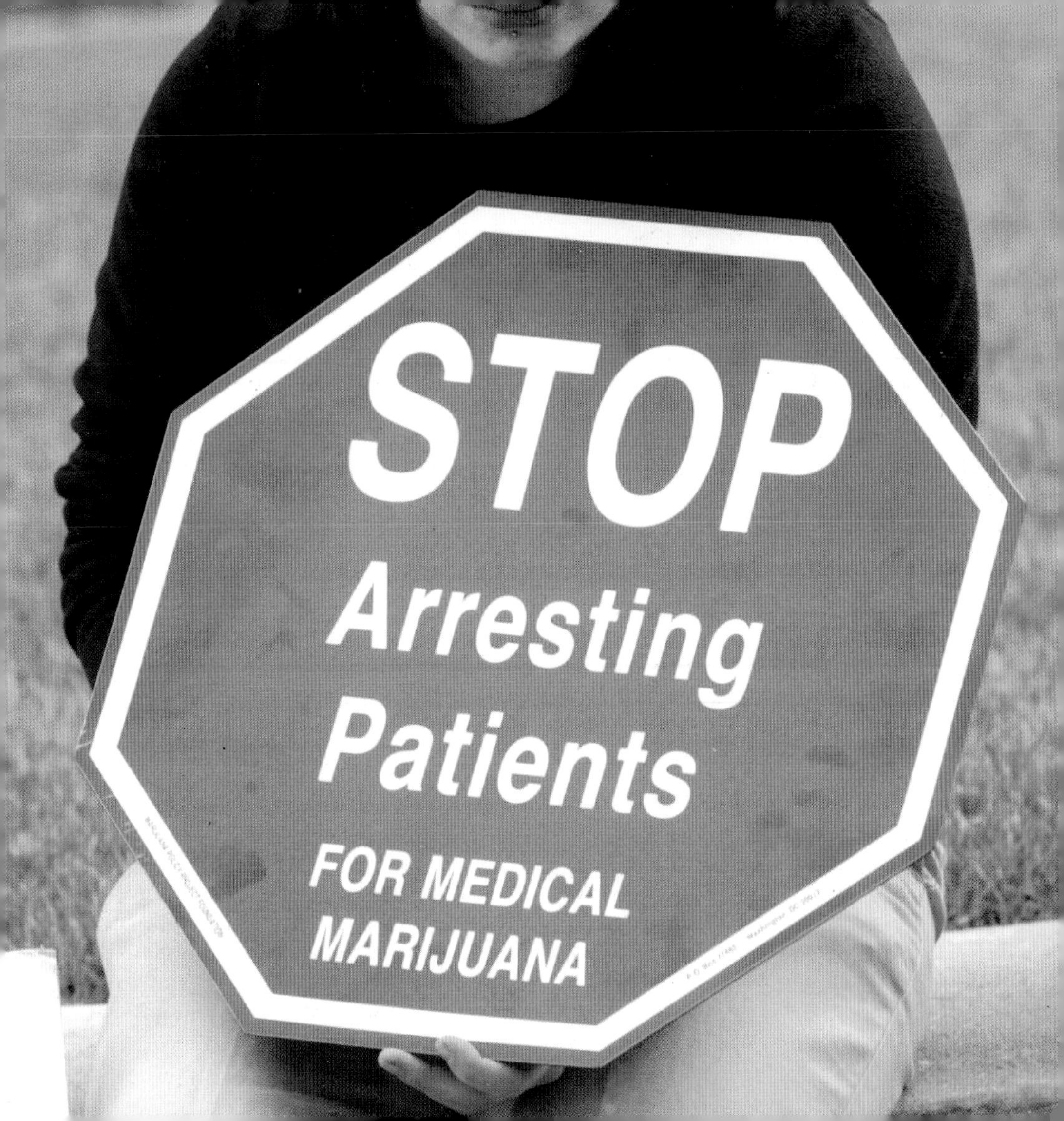
STOP
Arresting
Patients
FOR MEDICAL
MARIJUANA

The dreaded 'whitey'

A further criticizm levelled against cannabis is the potential danger of its psychoactive properties. And some medical experts have expressed concern that these dangers have escalated in recent years in the wake of the sensimilla revolution which significantly raised THC levels in skunk grass. While most potheads applauded this development wholeheartedly, some medics argued that it aggravated symptoms such as short-term memory loss and anxiety. And it is undoubtedly true that sometimes, rather than getting high and mellowing out, cannabis users can become prone to paranoia and panic attacks. Such episodes are often referred to as 'whiteys' – effectively the bad acid trips of the cannabis world. Whitey sufferers go pale – hence the name – as well as losing their balance and sense of coordination. Unpleasant headrushes and vertigo are often accompanied by dryness of mouth, nausea and ringing in the ears. Whiteys most commonly occur among inexperienced cannabis consumers and probably the best way of tackling them is to hide under the duvet until they go away.

Cannabis psychosis

A more serious condition is that of cannabis psychosis. Basically this is a case of regular psychosis that is exacerbated or in some cases even triggered by consumption of cannabis. In such cases, cannabis's psychoactive THC content serves as an irritant in awakening certain dormant mental conditions. So, for people with a predisposition to psychotic illnesses, cannabis consumption may induce a whole range of nasty side-effects such as delusions, mood swings and hallucinations. For those unlucky enough to be prone to psychosis, in whatever form, it is best to avoid cannabis altogether.

Cannabis clubs

Medical marijuana has become a particularly controversial issue in the US recently, especially so in California.

This is because in California, along with several other American states, local legislation enacted in the mid-1990s allows people to grow or possess small amounts of marijuana for medical use so long as they have obtained permission from their doctors first. Following the introduction of this legislation a group called the Cannabis Action Network (CAN) was launched in San Francisco in 1996. The purpose of CAN was to set up a number of 'cannabis clubs' around the Bay Area to provide medical users with a way of buying their marijuana without having to resort to black market channels. Apart from regular marijuana, the clubs also sell space cakes and tinctures. Such was the success of this initiative that a network of 20 such clubs soon sprang up. Although strictly speaking it is only

Right: Prescription-grade marijuana can be consumed in a variety of ways. It is seen here as cakes, cookies and regular grass.

ARCIA
23/97

Amigo Brand

MEDICAL
MARIJUANA

100% Medical Marijuana

Cannabis Club
Price: $
Grade:
3.5 Grams

4A
$$$

mariju

Cannabis Club
Price: $
Grade:
3.5 Grams

3A

ix Brand

MEDICAL MARIJUANA
LEMON SQUARES
BY BUYERS' CLUB
DOSAGE 1/4-1/2 BAR

BLAST OFF BANANA BREAD
ORGANIC - VEGAN
*whole wheat flour, *succanat
*baking powder, *bananas, *applesauce,
*canola oil, *outdoor buds!

MEDICAL MARIJUANA
SPICE CAK
BY CULTIVATORS'
DOSAGE: 1/4-1/2

MEDICAL MARIJUANA
by CULTIVATORS CLUB
DOSAGE: 1/4-1/2 BAR

Chronic
Vegan
Cannabis C

Ingredients: Organic
Organic Sucanat, Orga
Safflower Oil, Organic
Soy Milk, Corn Starch
Vanilla, Sea Salt

the possession – and not the trade – of marijuana that is allowed under Californian state law, the clubs were regarded as providing a valuable public service and continued to operate with impunity for a period of time. CAN's activities received the full backing of NORML and other pro-cannabis campaigning groups and it was hoped that these Bay Area branches would eventually go on to serve as prototypes for cannabis clubs in other American states as and when they enacted legislation along the enlightened Californian lines.

Unfortunately, however, the liberal legislative attitude of the Californians ran counter to federal laws, thereby providing the national Drug Enforcement Agency with the pretext it needed in order to muscle in and bust the cannabis clubs. This it duly did in a series of raids carried out in 1997. Justifying the action taken by his men, an unrepentant DEA special agent Richard Meyer commented at the time, 'Any cultivation, possession and distribution of marijuana is illegal under federal law. We all know that federal law supersedes state law. It is our job to enforce those laws and we will.'

The upshot was that four men were charged under federal narcotics laws and one of the clubs – the Cannabis Cultivators Club – was temporarily shut.

Little has changed since that time, with the DEA and the cannabis clubs still locked in an antagonistic stalemate. A nationwide string of protests outside DEA offices in 2002 conspicuously failed to break the deadlock, while an insensitive and heavy-handed US Supreme Court ruling to the effect that possession of marijuana for medical reasons is no defence against prosecution under federal law has provided the DEA with yet further ammunition in its campaign of harassment against the beleaguered cannabis clubs.

The English patients

Variations on the theme of Californian cannabis clubs have also sprung up in towns and cities across the United Kingdom. The first and most widely publicised of these is the Dutch Experience café in Stockport in Lancashire. It was opened in 2001 by Colin Davies – a disabled cannabis campaigner – and attracted considerable media coverage. Although billed as an Amsterdam-style coffee shop, the Dutch Experience bears about as much resemblance to a coffee shop as the small provincial town of Stockport does to Amsterdam.

Despite the sensationalist media coverage surrounding its opening, cannabis was not actually on sale at the cafe and nor was it intended as a bolthole for potheads who wanted to while away a few hours getting stoned while chilling to the sounds of Jimi Hendrix.

What Davies had in mind was more along the lines of a day centre where people suffering from a variety of different medical conditions could drop by to smoke their own dope in a sympathetic environment.

In the event, the café was raided on its opening day and Davies was busted for smoking a joint in the full media glare. Defiantly unrepentant at his subsequent hearing, the authorities decided to make an example of Davies, who was held on remand for seven months before being sentenced to three years in 2002. To a large extent Davies can be said to have engineered his own marijuana martyrdom as a publicity stunt to draw attention to the plight of those using dope for genuinely medical reasons. And he has been successful in this. The Dutch Experience has continued to open for business in Davies's absence without attracting any further raids by the authorities and has since spawned a string of similar style venues across the UK. And in a further promising development for the future of medical marijuana in the UK, a company called GW Pharmaceuticals was recently granted permission to cultivate 40,000 plants for medical purposes.

Green light for change

Official attitudes also appear to be softening towards the recreational use of cannabis in the UK, as was recently demonstrated by a scheme piloted in the South London borough of Lambeth – an area that has long been notorious for high levels of drug-related crime. With police resources stretched to the limit, Commander Brian Paddick decided to initiate a 'softly, softly' approach to minor cannabis offences, thereby freeing up his manpower and resources to tackle more serious drug-related crimes arising from the use of hard drugs like crack and heroin. So successful did the scheme prove to be that the government now seems set on extending it nationally by downgrading the classification of cannabis from a Class B to a Class C drug. Promising news indeed.

Sense and sensimilla

However, perhaps even more important than changes to the legal status of cannabis around the world have been changes in people's attitude towards the drug. There have been two principal causes for this, each closely linked to the other.

The first has been the explosion in popularity of sensimilla and the resulting empowerment of homegrowers. The coming of sensimilla effectively cut out the criminal middlemen who previously controlled the cannabis trade and tarnished its reputation by association. Shedding its stigma of criminality, cannabis has become increasingly ubiquitous and its use more acceptable. The growth in cottage industries of homegrown sensimilla has also significantly enhanced quality control – by growing the stuff themselves, potheads can rest assured that the gear they're skinning up hasn't been tampered with or adulterated. This, likewise, has significantly widened its appeal.

The second catalyst for change has been the internet. By pooling cannabis resources and opening up opportunities for trade in seeds and other growing paraphernalia, the internet has become the prime catalyst in promoting the sensimilla revolution worldwide.

A Web of Weed

Tap the word 'cannabis' into any major search engine and you will come up with almost a million hits. A quick scan reveals all manner of cannabis-themed archives, libraries, magazines and newsletters.

There are cannabis foundations, cannabis alliances, cannabis political parties, cannabis lobbyists, cannabis medical research groups, cannabis cookery clubs, cannabis coffee shop directories, cannabis Christian groups, cannabis bulletin boards, cannabis chat rooms… the permutations are positively endless.

However, the net's greatest achievement of all in propagating cannabis culture has undoubtedly been in spreading the gospel of sensimilla. The technical know-how required to grow sensimilla is now readily available to anyone with access to the web.

And it's not just the know-how that the net is providing – it's also the wherewithal. Demand for homegrowing products, and especially top-quality stabilised seeds, is now at an all-time high and the internet has proved itself the ideal medium for supplying that demand.

Seeds are premium priced, offer high margins, weigh next to nothing and take up no space – the perfect mail-order product. Some countries – notably Britain, the Netherlands, Italy, Portugal and Canada – are laxer in regard to the trade than others. Added to which, the mail-order companies are often protected by legal loopholes. In the UK, for instance, there is no law against selling or possessing cannabis seeds. 'Cannabis seeds are not controlled under drug laws and we can't control people trading legal substances, even if they're being used to make illegal ones,' a home office spokesman recently admitted.

And even where there are laws against the trade, the anonymity of the net provides the perfect smoke screen for hindering detection by the authorities. 'Traditional investigative techniques can't be applied to the internet,' the UN-backed International Narcotics Control Board

Above: On-line headshops like this one at Everyonedoesit.com have been quick to catch on to the internet's potential.

recently reported. 'Sites can disappear overnight. Links can go on forever. Hosts may be in any country in the world.' And even when the authorities can theoretically track a business down, the cost of such an investigation often proves prohibitive and would far outweigh the relatively paltry penalties meted out by the courts if the case ever came up before them.

The upshot of this is that the lawmakers and enforcers have become powerless in the face of progress. There is now no stopping the march of marijuana. Sensimilla has swept away all obstacles in its path and potheads of the world have united to take control of their own destinies. Cannabis culture has finally come of age.

"Sites disappear overnight and the cost of an investigation often proves prohibitive"

"Make the most of hemp
seed. Sow it everywhere"

George Washington

Glossary

AFGHANISTAN The country. Producer of fine Afghani hash.

AMSTERDAM City in the Netherlands where the smoking of marijuana has been de-criminalised in certain areas and designated places.

AUSTRALIAN Oh-so-blatant 'secret' code referring to the abbreviation 'Oz' for 'ounce'.

BAGGY A plastic bag for storing weed.

BAT PRESSING System using bats or mallets to press cannabis into hashish.

BEGIJ Indian word for grass and hash.

BLACK A form of hashish.

BLIM-BURN The physical evidence left on clothes, seats, and sometimes skin, caused by burning particles of hashish (see HOT ROCKS).

BLUNT A big fat spliff made by rolling pure weed in a cigar leaf.

BOGART After 'Humphrey Bogart', and used when someone holds onto a spliff for longer than they really ought to!

BONG A water-cooled pipe.

BORDER HASH The hash made on the border between Pakistan and Afghanistan. Particularly prevalent on the Western market during the late 1970s.

BUBBLE-GUM The name given to a particularly strong and fruity strain of skunk.

BUSTED Caught red-handed.

CAMBERWELL CARROT A joint of prodigious proportions requiring 12 skins to build. Invented by Danny the dealer of *Withnail & I* fame.

CANNABINOIDS Molecules such as the psychoactive THC that are unique to cannabis plants.

CANNABIS Genus name of marijuana and hemp plants.

CANNABIS INDICA Squat species of cannabis originating from Afghanistan and often used in the West for the cultivation of sensimilla.

CANNABIS SATIVA The most common species of cannabis. Bushier and sweeter tasting than indica.

CHARAS Indian word for hand-rubbed hash.

CHILLUM Conical pipe originating from India that is smoked by cupping hands to form an air chamber.

COFFEE SHOP Amsterdam smoking den.

COTTON MOUTH Symptom of smoking cannabis, in which the mouth's saliva dries up.

CUCHIE Jamaican slang for a bong.

DEALER Person who sells cannabis.

DOOBIE Slang name for a joint.

DOPE Slang for cannabis.

DRAW English slang for cannabis.

FARMER'S DAUGHTER Rhyming slang for a 'quarter' of an ounce of weed or hash.

FIRING UP Puffing pot in an energetic manner, especially through an Indian chillum pipe.

FIX Old term used in conversation to say you wanted to get wasted. Used in reference to not only marijuana but also harder drugs.

GANJA Indian word for marijuana. Also used in Jamaica.

GEAR General classification for cannabis of all types; sometimes used to refer to harder drugs too.

GIGGLES, THE Hysterical laughter is a symptom of smoking grass.

GIRAFFE Rhyming slang meaning a 'half' an ounce; also known as a 'Steffi Graff'.

GLAUCOMA Medical condition of the eye that can respond well to cannabis treatment.

GRASS Colloquial name for marijuana.

GREEN Another name for weed of all sorts, due – obviously – to the colour.

GRINDER A small circular device in two halves. used for grinding weed.

HAND PRESSING Labour-intensive way of making hashish by rubbing marijuana resin glands between the hands.

HASHISH Marijuana preparation that involves pressing together cannabis resin glands which have been obtained from female flowers by sieving.

HEAD RUSH Overwhelming dizziness and sense of euphoria that results from excessive indulgence

HEMP Fibre obtained from marijuana plants.

HIGH State of enlightenment attained through cannabis consumption.

HIT A puff of cannabis.

HOOKAH Middle Eastern water pipe.

HOT KNIVES Method of smoking hash.

HOT ROCKS Red-hot hash embers that drop from the end of a joint.

HYDROPONICS System used for growing plants indoors that employs a neutral growing medium other than soil.

ICE-O-LATOR New Dutch-pioneered system of manufacturing hash from sensimilla.

INFLORESCENCES Male and female flowers of the cannabis plant.

JOINT Cannabis cigarette. Joints can be either rolled with pure grass or mixed with tobacco. Pure single-skin joints

favour a mix of cannabis and tobacco, often rolled on a larger scale using three or more papers stuck together.

JUNGLI The Indian name for marijuana growing wild.

KIF A Moroccan preparation used in pipes combining female cannabis flowers mixed with dark tobacco.

LOADING The practice of concentrating more weed in a certain area of a spliff.

MANICURING Trimming outer leaves around marijuana buds.

MARIJUANA The Mexican name for grass.

MESH Circular metal filter inserted into the bowl of hash pipes.

POLLEN Resin glands obtained by threshing dried female flowers. Often the name incorrectly used in the US to refer to hash.

POT Western slang word for any form of cannabis preparation.

POTHEAD A cannabis aficionado.

PUFF Slang for cannabis.

RASTAFARIAN Dreadlocked member of a Jamaican sect who smokes a lot of ganja.

REEFER A slang name for a joint that was particularly popular during the 1930s and 1940s.

RESIN Thick sticky liquid produced by plants. Cannabis resin contains the psychoactive THC compound.

ROACH Joint filter made out of coiled strip of cardboard.

SADHU Wandering holy man of India who reveres the Hindu god Lord Shiva and regards cannabis as a sacrament.

SCORE Slang for the purchase of an amount of cannabis.

SENSIMILLA From the Spanish, literally meaning without seed. Name used to describe unfertilised female flowers.

SHIT Archaic slang word for cannabis.

SHOTGUN Aka a blowback. Way of smoking a joint whereby a toker takes burning end of joint into mouth and blows a jet of smoke through the roach into companion's mouth.

SIEVING Method of filtering THC-rich resin glands from dried female cannabis by threshing over a screen.

SKIN Slang name for a rolling paper.

SKUNK Generic name often used to denote sensimilla.

SMOKE-IN Gathering of potheads.

SPACE CAKE Cup cakes that have been baked using cannabis ingredients.

SPACE SHAKE Milk-based smoothie laced with cannabis.

SPLIFF Another name for a joint. Also sometimes incorrectly used as a slang name for a rolling paper.

STONED Effects of taking cannabis.

STONER A regular cannabis consumer.

THC Tetrahydrocannabinol is the primary psychoactive element found in cannabis.

TINCTURE A popular 19th-century way of preparing cannabis by dissolving its THC content in alcohol.

TOKE A puff of a joint or a cannabis pipe.

TRICHOM A plant hair often bristling with cannabis resin glands.

VAPORISER Generic name for a breed of revolutionary new pipes that produce a steam vapour rather than conventional smoke. This 'steam smoke' is said to be twice as potent and flavoursome as regular smoke.

WEED Slang name for marijuana.

ZONKED State of inebriation following excessive cannabis consumption.

Websites

There are more than a million sites devoted to cannabis. The following half dozen are as good a starting point as any and provide gateway links to many others.

www.cannabis.com

www.cannabisculture.com

www.erowid.org

www.cannabisnews.com

www.druglibrary.org

www.everyonedoesit.com

Bibliography

Andrews, George & Vinkenoog, Simon: *The Book of Grass – An Anthology of Indian Hemp*, New York, Grove Press, 1967

Barret, Leonard E Senior: *The Rastafarians*, Boston, Beacon Press, 1997

Boon, Marcus: *The Road Of Excess*, Harvard University Press, 2002

Cherniak, Laurence: *The Great Books of Hashish*, Volume I of nine, California, And/Or Press, 1979

Clarke, Robert C: *Hashish!*, Red Eye Press, California,1998

Davenport-Hines, Richard: *The Pursuit of Oblivion*, London, Weidenfeld & Nicolson, 2000

Frank, Mel: *Marijuana Grower's Inside Guide*, California, Red Eye Press, 1988

Green, Jonathon: *Cannabis*, London, Pavilion, 2002

Herer, Jack: *The Emperor Wears No Clothes*, Quick American Archives, 1979

King, Jason: *The Cannabible*, California, Ten Speed Press, 2001

Ludlow, Fitzhugh: *The Hasheesh Eater*, New York, Harper and Brothers, 1857

Marks, Howard: *Mr Nice*, London, Secker & Warburg, 1996

Matthews, Patrick: *Cannabis Culture*, London, Bloomsbury, 1999

Mezzrow, Milton & Wolfe Bernard: *Really The Blues*, New York, Random House, 1946

Rosenthal, Ed: *Marijuana Growers Handbook*, California, Quick American Publishing Company, 1984

Shapiro, Harry: *Waiting For The Man*, London, Mandarin, 1990

Sloman, Larry: *Reefer Madness: The History of Marijuana in America*, New York, Bobbs-Merrill, 1979

Solomon, David: *The Marihuana Papers*, New York, Bobbs-Merrill, 1966

Watts, Alan W: *The Joyous Cosmology*, New York, Random House, 1965

Acknowledgements

Editor's note

The production of this book would not have been possible without the assistance, advice and co-operation of many people, most of whom gave of their time both freely and generously. Thanks are due, in no particular order, to: Lorna, Peter and Mercedes at Amsterdam's Cannabis College for putting us on track; to Mila Jansen, Steven van der Veer and Robbie Terris at the Pollinator Company; to Eric and Arwin at The Dampkring for opening early and letting us take over their coffee shop for a morning; to Rene for skinning up with skill under the lights; to Sander at Homegrown Fantasy; to Neil our intrepid photographer who kept his cool when everything else was going up in smoke; to Paul at Grade Design for patience, good humour and a little expert guidance; to Mark at Everyonedoesit.com for advice and for supplying pictures; to the ever-glamorous Sarah Ford for cookery tips; to Mouldypea for rolling an array of spectacular joints; to Richard Kemplay at Bobcat Press and finally to Chris and Will at Chrysalis for both foresight and remarkable patience.